Sacred Story

Sacred Story

Finding God in the Ordinary

Daryl M. Knudeson

two worlds press

© 2013 by Daryl M. Knudeson
Published by Two Worlds Press,
a division of Two Worlds Media
Brush Prairie, WA

Printed in the United States of America

ISBN-13: 978-1494860585

ISBN-10: 1494860589

Dedication

For Sean, Casey, Sasha, Brooke and Bailey.
May your eyes always be open to His Presence;

And for Uncle Ken (Unkie Dunk)
because your enthusiasm about my life story
gave me the courage to write.

The spiritual [person] never believes

circumstances to be haphazard,

or thinks of his life as secular or sacred;

he sees everything…as the means of securing

the knowledge of Jesus Christ.

Oswald Chambers,
My Utmost for His Highest

Contents

Preface

I've long admired Jesus' method of conveying spiritual truth about the kingdom of God through the use of earthly stories. Speaking in parables, He illustrated valuable lessons to those who followed Him by drawing upon common or familiar human experiences. It wasn't until my late thirties that I began to realize many of the situations from my otherwise common life had deeper implications which pointed to spiritual truths. When I took the time to be still and listen to the guidance of the Scriptures and the Holy Spirit, I found heavenly messages tucked away in the ordinary, and sometimes extraordinary, circumstances of my life. It is with a grateful heart that I record these lessons with the hope that you too will look for the parables in your own life and give glory to God for His intimate involvement in our everyday lives.

Acknowledgments

Behind every completed work there are many individuals who play a vital role in helping to transform what is in the heart and mind of the author into pages which can communicate the story or concept to others. It is my privilege to extend my thanks to those who took time from their busy lives to read sections of my manuscript and offer their thoughts, suggestions and encouragement. To Jettie Omdahl, your love of grammar and your constant enthusiasm for this work kept my head above water more than you realize. To the Rep Board at International Renewal Ministries: Dennis Fuqua, Jody Mayhew, Glen Weber, Howard Boyd, Steve Hall, Richard Williams and Steve Zimmerman, your lives are filled with service to others yet you honored me through sharing your precious time. To Sherry Myers, Natasha Padilla, Terrie Gerner, Tegan VandenBosch, Julie Tadema and Bob and Wanda Mason, your eagerness to pray, read, and dialogue with me about the stories gave me the sense of how this book would impact others. To my family, Gloria and Herb Andrews, Shirley Knudeson and Ken and Joan Robinson, you lovingly read every word and kept asking if I was finished; I needed the push forward! To Dan Mayhew at Two Worlds

Media, you did all the necessary work of turning the manuscript into a book. And to my husband, Jason, you were there to read the first print of every story, and always believed I could write. Without each of you this book would not be written.

Daryl Knudeson
December 23, 2013
Albuquerque, New Mexico

Introduction

Story. What comes to mind when you hear that word? Does it evoke childhood memories of snuggling close to a parent, eyes wide in wonder as you hung on every word? Perhaps it brings to mind the drama of a life well lived, or a person whose experiences or accomplishments inspired you to pursue a different path. Have you considered the narrative being written through the daily events of your life?

Each of us has a story, be it a lost romance and missed opportunity echoing Gone with the Wind, a sobering journey of individual triumph akin to Chariots of Fire, or a tear-jerker right from the pages of The Titanic. It is within our own story that we can find the heart of God conveying the incredible truth about His love for us.

My goal in sharing these personal stories is to motivate you, the reader, to explore the everyday situations and search for clues creatively buried within the norms of daily living. As you ponder the Scripture passages included with each of the forty stories, reflect upon God's presence within the pages of your day, and pause in reverence to thank the One who desires to communicate that He is near.

Used as a daily devotional or to provoke treasured communion found in sharing your story with others, may you experience the blessing of seeing God more clearly through the lens of a grateful heart.

Mirrored in Sand

Secretly delighted to be walking solo on this stretch of beach along the Oregon Coast, I relished the cool sea breeze against my face and the repetitious crashing of the waves upon the shore. The sun, still cradled beneath the hillside to my left, barely exposed a misty horizon down the shoreline. Seagulls, determined to catch their breakfast in the pre-dawn quiet, eyed me suspiciously. The enormous rock appropriately called Haystack, stood like a sentinel in the distance, its front edge heavily immersed by the tide.

Growing up near the Coast of Southern California and spending a large chunk of my teenage life engrossed in sun and sea, I developed a special affinity for the ocean; however, this particular length of sand represented more than youth's exuberance, or the emergence into womanhood noticed by those who frequented the bikini clad beaches in the mid-seventies. Well into my forties and seasoned by time's passage, I cherished this particular place for what it represented to my spiritual growth. Though as a pastor's wife I had spent many hours praying and teaching the Bible to others, I heard God when I walked here—not audibly, although that wouldn't have surprised me, but God seemed to unwrap my tangle of thoughts and emotions and I always went home understanding the direction of my life more clearly after spending time here.

Pulling my jacket tighter against the breeze, I fingered a scrap of paper in my pocket I had picked up in the church parking lot the day before I left for the beach. It had a single phrase written on it: God created man in His own image. Perhaps it had fallen from a child's hand on her way to the car after Sunday school, but for some reason it struck me and I silently prayed, "Why is this significant Lord? Teach me." Still in thought, I looked out across the sea and then down at the sand just in front of my feet. As the wave receded, I was surprised to find that the sand mirrored the image of Haystack Rock——a bit uneven, but there was no doubt what reflection I was looking at. The phrase "I created you in My image" danced across my thoughts. Looking up at the true rock, I smiled at the sense of love I felt in knowing this fact.

I have learned over the years that when a particular verse from Scripture impacts you it is well worth your time to reflect upon it. When the same verse finds its way onto your radar more than once in that same week, it is wise to stop and pray about it. "What is it Lord? Why is this verse significant for me?" I asked. Continuing slowly up the beach, I felt the imposing presence of Haystack, and noticed that the western sky was no longer the deep blue which precedes sunrise. The sea was calm, and the waves rolled in steady succession, threatening my shoes.

Bending over to collect a shell, I came face to face with the reflection of the huge rock once again; this time the image was much clearer as the increased light revealed more of its true image. Intent on understanding the parable unfolding in progression like the waves, I quickly looked up. The rock appeared as quiet and immoveable as always, but my eyes felt drawn to look just beyond, to the far side where the incoming tide first reaches it.

I felt the pace of my heart quicken as I watched the waves crashing against the outlying section of the immense rock; they pounded relentlessly, spray shooting up into the air only to return foaming and swirling onward to the beach. But the rock stood firm. No amount of pressure from the waves could move it. The riotous turmoil in the sea touched its base, but it had no effect upon the rock whatsoever; it continued to stand firm. My mind, racing to catch up with the emotion of my heart, clung in appreciation to this oceanic lesson: "The closer you move toward Me, the greater the intensity of the turmoil. The nearer you are to Me, the greater the war for your peace, for your true life. Expect it My child. Do not run from it."

I stood in complete wonder as I watched the drama evolve: waves thundering persistently, only to be deflected by the enormity of the rock until the full impact of the lesson reached a permanent resting place within me: "In the world you will have tribulation, but be of good cheer, I have overcome the world" (John 16:33 NKJV). It was several moments before I turned to walk back to my hotel.

In the seconds it took for me to turn back into the direction I had come from, I felt a strange sensation on the left side of my face which was now adjacent to the rock. Something tangible rested against my cheek and I reached up to touch it. The pull to turn and catch a glimpse was irresistible.

Even at my human best I have a limited perspective of the greatness of God, and it was no different this particular morning. The picture displayed before me was breathtaking: The sun had just crested the hillside, transforming the glistening shore into a mirror of massive proportions, but Haystack, the Rock, had also been transformed into a radiant, golden tower gleaming with a radiance beyond words. Just beneath it on the wet sand was its image, cast so perfectly that my eyes beheld even the tiny, nesting birds on the rock face! Every crevice, every shadow was mirrored with exact detail in the sand directly at my feet.

As the tears fell in reverence, my spirit gleaned part two of God's special lesson: "Someday you will reflect me so perfectly that no one will be able to tell that it is you, for they will see Me. Never let your limitations or the suffering you experience blind you to the fact that you are created in My image for this reason, so the world can see Me. Expect It, My child. And do not run from it."

Celestial Possibility

"One thing I do, forgetting those things which are behind and reaching forward to those things which are ahead, I press toward the goal for the prize of the upward call of God in Christ Jesus."

Philippians 3:13-14 (NKJV)

Those who live with a serious disease such as cancer face the daily challenge of riding an emotional roller coaster. Months, perhaps years roll by as they navigate the twists and turns facing them on the road to recovery. Painfully, sometimes that road culminates at a dead-end, betraying all the hopes, mocking the courage and shattering the dreams. Silently observing one another, both patient and caregiver travel into the realm of the unknown, exerting vast amounts of energy as they plot a course through the doctor visits, medications and surgeries. We were three and a half years into our own journey through leukemia, successfully riding down the highway of remission for the better part of that time when the sudden U-turn in my first husband's health brought us to our knees, desperate for intervention.

It was the week between Christmas and New Year's when the hemorrhaging began—with Gary's doctor out of town for the holidays we resorted to dialing 9-1-1 in hope that they could stop the bleeding. Within three hours we found ourselves at the hospital filling out the admittance paperwork. His platelet count had dropped dangerously low, and there could be no stopping the hemorrhage until he had a transfusion. The dreaded inevitable came to pass—we were told to prepare to stay until Gary's doctor returned from vacation.

Sitting in the small hospital room on New Year's Eve, I listened carefully to the doctor explain why intravenous chemotherapy was our only chance for a return to remission. It would require four continuous, separate but simultaneous IV drips in the week ahead. Struggling with the news, we agreed to place Gary under the scrutiny and care of the oncology team, but we placed our hopes in God. We had various conversations with the doctor concerning the possibilities, but we knew the risks were high and it would take a miracle to bring about the desired outcome. Bracing ourselves for our darkest journey yet, we waited for the team to insert a port-a-cath in Gary's chest to provide the pathway for the synchronized flow of cancer-fighting chemotherapy. I remember commenting to the nurse during the first several days of chemo that my husband looked and felt so good it was hard to believe his body had been absorbing the continuous current of such potent chemicals. Turning to me and lowering her voice she replied, "Sweetie, this is the calm before the storm."

There is a point when the human soul must weed through the conflicting emotions and thoughts and pursue those things that are true and right—a pursuit of the things that anchor us to all that is real in this life and hoped for beyond it. Week number three in the hospital hurled Gary into a nightmarish existence between the fear of dying in the hospital away from family, and the realization that perhaps the time for relishing in the blessings of life was running out. On an especially dark night around three o'clock in the morning he had had enough, and without observance he slipped out of his hospital room and stealthily made his way past the nurse's station. His goal was the elevator; and as he pushed the button, which would carry him to freedom (home), he was intercepted by a nurse who had approached from another hallway. Gently ushering him back to his room, she quickly dialed our number. With no one to relieve my night watch over our children, I made a call to our pastor who, after hearing my panicked plea, assured me that he would be at the hospital within minutes.

Early the following morning I was summoned to the hospital at the request of the doctor. Stepping through the elevator doors, I immediately recognized his profile standing in front of the nurse's station. Glancing my way, he signaled me to come over, and setting his clipboard on the counter, turned to face me. It was then that I noticed the back-fill of tears in his eyes, and the solemn expression covering his normally happy countenance. His faith in God had seen him through many differing outcomes in many different patients over the years, and it was this faith that now glued his feet to the floor in front of me in order to share what he obviously had a hard time uttering. Reaching out to enfold me in his arms, he shivered and then whispered in my ear, "I'm so sad. I can't do anything to save my friend." Time stood still, and I willed myself to wrap my brain around his words, but grief had shrouded my heart and I steadied myself against the counter. "I've tried everything, and I'm afraid the cancer is too far along now to go back into remission. He is desperate and wants to go home, so I am giving him an eight hour pass to come home for the day. Promise me you will be very careful until he returns here tonight."

Rounding the corner to our house, I realized that our drive had been in silence. He was anxious to be in the surroundings he'd left nearly a month earlier, but mostly he wanted to be in the presence of our children. Backing into the driveway, I told him not to try to get out of the car without my help. The formerly capable and independent man did not argue with me, but instead leaned his head back against the seat to wait. Arm-in-arm we slowly walked down the path to the front door. Still holding on to me as I turned the key in the lock, he closed his eyes as the front door swung open. In a moment of relief and urgency, he let go of my arm and took his first step up the threshold and into the entry way. His legs, weakened from the chemo and the inactivity, gave way and he fell onto the floor in a heap. Not knowing what to do I put my hand on his shoulder, but in the few seconds it had taken to hit the ground, Gary had already made a conscious resignation which spoke silently and helplessly in his eyes as he looked up at me. "I can't do this, can I?" he murmured. After four hours in the recliner situated about five feet from the front door, he asked me to return him to the hospital.

Twenty-two years later the image of his face looking up at me still brings me to tears. Months after Gary's death, his doctor revealed to me that the loss of human dignity is by far the most difficult grief to bear, and the one which takes the longest to heal.

I think it was hope that led Gary to attempt what his doctor and I knew were near impossibilities. He believed that being home with his family would somehow bring the possibility of healing, if not in his body then at least in his soul. I think too, from his vantage point on the floor of our entry way, something shifted within his understanding and he no longer hung his future upon the fleeting possibilities of earth. Instead he made the decision to hang his hat upon something far more promising: "With God, all things are possible" (Matthew 19:26 NIV).

The Black One

Jesus said, "Let the little children come to Me, and do not hinder them, for the kingdom of heaven belongs to such as these."

Matthew 19:14 (NIV)

It was one of those rare and incredibly warm spring days in Oregon, and I had left the kitchen door open to let both the sun and warmth inside. Catching the scent of lilacs and iris on the gentle breeze, I leaned back against the counter, blissfully content in knowing the damp, bone-chilling winter had passed once again. Soft beams of sunlight cascaded through the openings between curtain panels, highlighting the swirling, weightless dust. The children were playing just outside the door beneath the shelter of our covered driveway. Spreading the last of the peanut butter across a piece of homemade bread, I heard the familiar sounds of our daughter, her little voice carrying on a conversation with no one in particular. Setting the sandwiches on the table, my mother's instinct seemed to engage. Taking a peek out the kitchen window to take inventory of my little charges, those same instincts shifted into overdrive as I beheld a most surprising spectacle at the far end of the driveway.

At three years of age, Casey was about a head taller than the moveable fence across the end of the driveway. Her back was facing the house, and perched directly opposite her little cherub face was the largest black raven I had ever seen. My heart froze as visions of Alfred Hitchcock's movie *The Birds* flashed across my mind. Moving quickly to the kitchen door and then, ever so slowly, I made my way outside to rescue my unsuspecting child. I could tell by her relaxed stance that she did not share my anxiety. Unable to calmly issue a warning, I inched closer. The massive bird cocked his head in my direction, suspicious of my stealth approach. Several feet from my goal, I realized that this feathered intruder had some sort of band around his left foot, the plastic type one uses to secure a cord or a bundle. Stopping to recalculate my final approach, a smile found its way to my face as I could hear the conversation taking place between child and animal: "Hi birdie, birdie, birdie! You beautiful, birdie, birdie, birdie! What you name, birdie, birdie, birdie?"

There was no apparent tension in anyone but me, so I let my guard down a bit and gently pulled Casey back to a safer distance. Our son, Sean, caught sight of the situation and joined us at the fence. It quickly became obvious that this bird was familiar with people. Still, his enormous beak could easily inflict injury, so I cautioned the kids to stay out of reach. My attempts to exercise parental discernment and due caution were quickly met with objections—from both bird and children. When the kids sat down on the driveway, the raven joined them, delighting everyone with his antics involving Sean's shoelaces. Moving from driveway to sandbox, sandbox to woodpile, the raven followed Sean and Casey closely and halted wherever they stopped. Of course, this thrilled the children to such an extent that the level of excitement increased to a near fevered pitch!

It was decided between the children that this was now their own special pet, and a pet must have a proper name. Without pretense, Sean thought carefully for the better part of ten seconds and then declared, "I know! Let's call him The Black One!" Casey, always the greatest fan of her big brother, dutifully shouted a resounding, "Yeah! The Black One!" And so it was decided. After several hours of laughter and joy, the grand finale came in the form of The Black One determining that Sean's head was the ideal perch from which to survey his tiny kingdom of children. Bird's claws are not the most comfortable adornments, especially to a piece of anatomy without much padding. Not to be conquered by any form of discomfort, Sean ran into the house shouting something about a "perfect idea" just before the screen door slammed.

Returning with a smile brighter than the sun, Sean stepped out onto the driveway in complete battle attire. From the shiny, plastic Roman breastplate to the shinier, green, plastic army helmet, Sean was prepared to overcome any obstacle in order to continue this close encounter with a most unusual friend. As the afternoon passed, the time came to retire, and with great struggle I managed to convince the children it was time for dinner. Surprisingly our visitor returned for the next several days before vanishing without a trace.

From time to time the kids and I reflect with amusement on those few special days over two decades ago. I keep a photo of Sean standing tall under the protection of that shiny, green army helmet—The Black One, unable to grip the plastic with his claws, flapping ferociously to avoid sliding off. We will never know the reason for the visit, but the memories of that unexpected encounter will last, and undoubtedly find their way into our conversation again.

Because of the innocence and trust of a three year old, a treasured meeting took place—one that I would have probably shooed away out of fear and the unwillingness to take a risk. In my adult, mature reasoning I would have concluded the whole matter as foolish, dangerous, an accident waiting to happen. And I would have missed the beauty, simplicity, and communion I gained with my kids because of our visitor.

There was another moment in time, over two thousand years ago, when Jesus gathered His disciples together to speak to them. They wanted to know what it took to become someone great in the kingdom of heaven. So Jesus took a small child, perhaps a three year old, and set him in the middle of the crowd. "Truly, I say to you, unless you are converted and become as little children, you shall not enter the kingdom of heaven" (Matthew 18:3 NASB). Jesus wasn't referring to adults reverting back to childish behaviors. He was communicating the secret of humility which is a requirement of accepting the truth of God. Unless we have the innocence, the unguarded heart, the simple faith which characterizes little children in our own hearts, we are at risk of shooing away the evidence of God's treasured encounters with His children—and the beauty and simplicity of His visits.

Insect Appeal

Taken by surprise at the vast expanse of humanity which lay beneath our plane, I leaned back into my less than comfortable seat as the pilot announced our final descent into Mexico City. The grey-brown haze, evidence of severe air pollution, clung low over the city, exchanging a colorful palate for muted tones. Adjusting myself in order to gain a different perspective of the urban sprawl, I wondered how the average citizen coped with the daily challenge of navigating the unending labyrinth of streets. Fifteen million people settled in this region of the country, many forced to live on the impoverished fringes of town after failing to find the better life they believed awaited them within the city.

Traveling with about twenty pastors, I was happy to have the company of two other females among the group. Signing up for this particular tour as an instructive, hands-on trip for ministers and their spouses, it was designed to educate us on the mission work associated with a unique ministry which brought relief aid to major disaster sites around the world. After several days visiting the ministry projects in Mexico City, we would board a bus and ride the three hundred-plus miles southeast into Oaxaca. The goal: To witness first hand some of the ongoing medical work which supported the indigenous Zapotec and Mixtec populations in the mountains surrounding the central portion of the state.

Impressive in scope, the medical team joined forces with their Mexican counterpart to better reach the inhabitants who lived in the grinding poverty plaguing the far reaches of the city. Arriving early in the morning in order to experience a typical day in the life of an at-risk child, we climbed out of our vans and onto the dusty streets which led into the heart of El Basurero, the Dump City. The school-after school center located a block from the edge of the dump was constructed with the typical grey cinder blocks, surrounded by a walled courtyard. The children (and sometimes the parents) arriving early enough to have a snack, attended classes until lunchtime, and then ate perhaps the only full meal of the day. Finishing the afternoon with songs and exercise, the children seemed to flourish in the loving and supportive atmosphere.

Within minutes of our arrival we found ourselves the focus of intense curiosity by the children, happily clinging to us and smiling shyly if spoken to in our mostly broken Spanish. Our heart-strings were pulled tightly by the end of the school day, but what we felt within the sparsely furnished classroom did not prepare us for the next hour as we entered the world of El Basurero. We learned that the residents of the dump cities often shared a similar story: Without work to sustain their families in the rural villages beyond the borders of Mexico City, they set their sights on the false promise of jobs in the thriving capital, only to encounter disappointed hopes and further poverty. Dumps were often the last effort to survive. Scraping together whatever would provide a makeshift house, the landscape was converted into an ocean of cardboard, plastic and scrap-metal dwellings. Sickly, malnourished dogs hovered around the edges of the dump while small children played noisily within sight of their homes made of someone else's discards. One fortunate woman who offered us a radiant smile held her small child in one arm while tending the meal she was preparing over her makeshift oil-barrel stove.

Sobered by the reality of how much these people lacked, the churning of painful truth began to burn a hole deep in my heart. Living in abject poverty, these beautiful people still had enough courage and hospitality to offer an obviously wealthier-than-themselves foreigner a gracious smile and a welcome greeting. Would I be so congenial in these circumstances, or had I become too accustomed to my current standard of living and the push to continue further up the economic ladder? Could I, without embarrassment, extend hospitality to a stranger-come-to-town on a mission to examine my sub-standard lifestyle? Though uncomfortable, I was grateful for the challenge to my self-imposed set of standards, promising myself to spend more time in the future evaluating how we spend our income and what portion we would set aside to, even if slightly, balance out this kind of discrepancy in the world. After attending the final event of the day, a graduation ceremony for six women who had completed sewing classes advanced enough to make them employable, we made the journey back to the hotel in thoughtful silence.

Morning arrived too soon, perhaps due to the restless night pondering the how and why of the obvious chasm between our life and life in El Basurero. The steady hum of our chartered bus wove its magic and I drifted in and out of sleep as we made our way south to Oaxaca. Aware of scratching only the surface of all we had come to see and experience, our walk through poverty had taken a toll on each heart and left us in a rather somber mood. After several attempts to lighten the atmosphere through singing some hymns, a commotion broke out in the back of the bus. Laughter, taking hold of the two in question, baited the majority to demand an account. During a brief shopping spree, one of the pastors had purchased a bag of considerable size filled with a traditional snack in this part of the world, chapulines. More accurately, deep-fried crickets. Spotting the bag-o-bugs, Manuel, our translator and guide, questioned the ability (or lack thereof) of the pastor who had purchased the contraband to eat them. Challenging the machismo of the masculine portion of our group, smiles quickly spread to the front of the bus.

One by one the male mystique over-powered common sense, each hombre endeavoring to out-do his colleagues in both vigor and humor. One by one the feminine fragment sank just a little lower in our seats, enjoying the comedy yet fearing we would soon become the next subjects. Our attempts at hiding did not go unnoticed as each of our husbands made their way toward us, gingerly carrying the fried corpse of a former ground-crawling, six-legged insect. Delighting in our instinct to squirm at the thought of one of the cadavers coming close to our faces, let alone touching our lips, the challenge was thus extended to the wives, and the bus roared with laughter. The crescendo of amusement struck a chord in me: The Little Sister Syndrome; instinctual in those who had an older brother who delighted in surprises of the insect type, and forever casting her into the category of helpless female after enduring countless bug-tortures. Shooting a glance at the other women, I sensed they too had encountered the early childhood persecution. But we were not children any more, and the weakness had been replaced by dignity (and maybe a slight case of pride) that refused to allow this mind-set to live on. With eyes shut tightly we submitted to the challenge and chewed, in my case gagged, with gusto until the crispy, pepperoni-tasting carcasses slid down our throats, followed by a full can of soda. If there is such a thing as machis-ma, we definitely had it!

Although needing to replace our sorrow with joy that day, each of us were touched to the far reaches of our hearts by the inconsistencies in life. The children we encountered the day before were no less important than our own. Their parent's efforts to support their families were no less noble than ours. Their desire to give their children opportunity resounded in their hearts as it did in ours. Yet there was a distinct difference that set them apart from a vast number of their wealthier North American neighbors: Contentment. Whether forced to live in a city of garbage, to rely upon the compassion of others to feed their children the only full meal of the day, or steadfastly pulling themselves out of poverty by beginning a small business sewing for those who no doubt had much more than they, each encounter with these remarkable people was full of grace and satisfaction—they had learned how to live without, and this fact freed them to live with a happiness and ease not often apparent in the United States.

In his letter to the Philippian church, the Apostle Paul spoke on the matter of living with contentment. His eloquent words point each of us, regardless of our current situation, to the key in finding peace no matter what hand life may deal us: "…for I have learned to be content whatever the circumstances. I know what it is to be in need, and I know what it is to have plenty. I have learned the secret of being content in any and every situation, whether well fed or hungry, whether living in plenty or in want. I can do everything through Him who gives me strength" (Philippians 4:11-13 NIV). For me, part of the lesson in this passage is the understanding that Paul faced both plenty and need in all of his earthly circumstances. It seems God did not withhold times of lack from Paul's life, which is sometimes contrary to Christian thinking today. Paul could then participate in this truth, which is foundational to authentic contentment: Times of lack are designed to draw us away from dependence upon ourselves and into dependence upon God, for His strength is sufficient and His storehouses are full.

Invisible Medicine

"For our light and momentary troubles are achieving for us an eternal glory that far outweighs them all."

2 Corinthians 4:16-18 (NIV)

Feeling exhausted from emotions now spent, I barely noticed the flash of headlights racing past me on the other side of the highway. Making this trip each night for the past month had taken its toll on my heart and my body, and I longed to be home in the comfort of my bed.

The honking horn from the car next to me snapped me out of my mental fog, forcing me to review the previous hour. The pale, icy green walls were not as distasteful to me as was the memory of the awful smells; smells that, unknown to me this night, would linger in my memory for decades. Struggling to focus on something else, my thoughts were held prisoner, chained securely to the recollections of this nightly ritual:

The long drive always ended in the same fashion, pulling into the enormous parking garage, searching for a slot as near to the elevators as I could find. The night air brisk and the icy east wind forcing its way into the smallest opening of my jacket. Hesitating in front of the glass doors, and then holding my breath in anticipation of the immediate rush of smells to my nose, coercing me to face the reality of my situation again.

Elevators quietly escort me to the desired floor, while small numbered signs with arrows direct my path to the correct room. Standing at the threshold I hear the quiet whir of machines, monitoring every rhythm of his heart. Four different IV bags, dripping silently, deposit chemicals through needles in his chest and arm. His labored breathing moves the lightweight, cotton blanket back and forth, reminding me of the receiving blankets I once wrapped the children in when they were newborns. Perhaps there is some underlying sense of peace in the room, but it is veiled by the ugly reality of sickness and death.

Stepping through the doorway, I make my way to the chair across the small room and survey the large scabs across his once handsome face—leftovers from the powerful doses of chemotherapy which had burned through his skin. I scarcely make it to the foot of the bed before his eyes open and the words—those words—begin to hurl from his mouth with the vengeance of a wounded lion. It is always more than I can bear, but from somewhere deep inside I am always compelled to stay, to endure this wrath, because deep in my heart I know he is afraid of what is to come. This is his way of facing the giants; his way of trying to push me away so that when the eventual reality comes into view maybe I won't care quite so much and it will make his absence more bearable.

The hour ends with an apology and the uncomfortable silence that invades when there is nothing left to say. I kiss his forehead and whisper "I love you," before he closes his eyes to find the solace of sleep once more.

Rounding the corner of our street, I welcomed the sight of our porch light shining in the darkness. My mom also made a nightly ritual: Keeping watch over our children so I was able to drive to the hospital, her presence upon my return a steady comfort and relief to me. Leaning into her embrace, I sensed that God was gently holding me as well, and I longed for something deeper to anchor me to this life; for something to break through the sorrow that gripped every waking moment.

With the children sleeping peacefully, I waved good-bye to my mom for the night and retreated to the living room to participate in still another ritual. This one, born of the need to grieve and to make sense of what I was experiencing, came with no disturbing images or distasteful smells, but rather with the assurance that I was involved in something larger than myself, yet common to many. Placing the headphones over my ears, I lay face down on the floor and turned the volume up on the stereo. As the music began to softly invite me to relax, God began to minister to my heart through the words of someone who had walked this same path. I felt my resistance lighten, tears pooling in the palms of my hands as my troubled mind worshipped the One who gives and takes away.

Though I had listened to this particular song each night since my husband's admittance into the hospital, I never tired of how the writer had penned my exact feelings. I drew a particular strength in knowing that someone else had felt what I felt, thought what I thought. Lying in the darkness I was able to come to terms with circumstances that were completely out of my control. My determination rose once more to be strong for him—to embrace hope in the midst of the impossible.

On one particular hospital visit I found our pastor sitting by my husband's bedside. Though still attached to numerous IV's, and weakened considerably from their powerful influence, he lie sleeping peacefully through the help of the morphine's pain numbing effects. Pastor Steve sat facing him, a slight smile visible across his face. "Gary saw an angel today. Right there at the foot of his bed. He sat straight up from a deep sleep to point him out to me." Speechless, I sat down on the small couch next to his chair. Taking my hand and squeezing it gently, he rose to leave. "He seems to have some peace now," Steve said, then turned and left the room.

If there were a method to avoid all suffering in this life, I would be first in line to sign up. But I have learned over the years that pain and suffering are not necessarily the double edged swords our culture claims them to be. We often try avoiding what appears negative because we associate pain and struggle with something bad. However, what if suffering is a tool to improve and mature us rather than destroy us? What if God, in His infinite wisdom and love, knows that it is through struggles that we learn to trust that He is present with us? What if, when circumstances are out of our control, we begin to understand that God is in control? What if through watching a loved one slip toward death, we begin to embrace the truth that there is more than this life? What if…?

The Unseen Altar

"Wash me thoroughly from my iniquity, and cleanse me from my sin."

Psalm 51:2 (NKJV)

Thick with moisture and insects, the air was palpable. Our chairs, forming a large circle as we sat under the slanted tin roof, offered a front row view of the women singing softly; others prayed earnestly as Latin women are apt to do. My attention, however, was fixed on young Rosa, a slim, dark haired woman cautiously making her way to the chair set in the center of the circle.

The women around the perimeter continued singing and praying while Rosa sat down, placing her elbows on her knees. Her lips moved silently, giving confirmation that she too was praying. Tears began to slowly wash down her face, her shoulders shaking now and then. Almost whispering, she said, "El Señor, lo siento. Límpiame" (Lord, I'm sorry. Cleanse me). A light rain began to fall without betraying the intimacy of the moment. Lifting her face toward the roof, she revealed the increase of her tears, now flowing steadily, and cried in a clear voice, "Padre, límpiame!" In the reverence of the moment I thought to myself, "Is it raining harder now?" I looked to my right, seeking affirmation from my friend. Turning to me, she widened her eyes in agreement.

As if from some deep cavern within her heart, Rosa's chest began to heave with emotion. Throwing her hands into the air she cried out in anguish, "Padre! Límpiame! Límpiame!" The peals of thunder that immediately followed startled everyone, but they were no match for the flood which suddenly fell from heaven. The deafening roar of the rain pounding against the tin roof supported the tempo of the splashes that shot out in all directions as they bounced off the ground. Looking again at my friend, we communed in silent amazement that this was not just a moment in time, it was a moment recorded in heaven: God Himself, hearing the cry of one of His daughters, condescended to quiet her aching heart.

The sense that we were spectators to something holy filled our chests, and the air felt almost too dense to breathe. Time seemed to stand still as the roar from the rain kept tempo with Rosa's sobs, and ours. Then gently, as if on cue from some unseen Director, the rain from heaven and from Rosa's heart began to subside.

Critics may say that it was just a coincidence. Skeptics may justify their doubts with rationalizations that God doesn't exist, let alone have time to hear the prayer of just one person. But as Rosa stood from her unseen altar, the radiance on her face spoke to any in doubt of a glorious encounter with her very real God.

Dying for Life

"…unless a grain of wheat falls into the earth and dies, it remains by itself alone; but if it dies, it bears much fruit."

John 12:24 (NASB)

The barren landscape boasted of its emptiness. Scattered shrubs clung obstinately to the parched soil, thirsty for the slightest drops of rain to sustain them for another day. The distant vista toyed with my imagination, seducing me with the delights of a sandy shore and azure sea just beyond. In every direction nature hung in a delicate balance within the unforgiving miles of this desert.

Occasionally, stark reminders of life's brevity dotted the scenery: A flash of red flesh torn open by vultures cloaked in feathered capes, their beaks resembling death's sickle in the hand of the Grim Reaper. A grave marker, painstakingly crafted from iron to withstand the fury of this place, ornate in design to declare the love once lavished upon Joe, who now rested eternally. An uprooted tumbleweed blowing across the road. The absence of other travelers on this stretch of highway only enhanced the bleak surroundings.

Lost in the barrage of gloomy thoughts, a particular Scripture verse from John's Gospel worked its way into my consciousness, "Unless a kernel of wheat falls to the ground and dies, it remains alone." The hard shell of the wheat kernel must first break open before it can release the life contained within it. Jesus' words illustrate a powerful metaphor for the paradox: Life requires death.

A new perspective jarred me from my dismal contemplating. The death of the desert animal sustained the life of the vultures. Perhaps Joe's grave marker had been placed there by his children, the fruit of his life refusing to forget him, erecting his memorial for all traveling this way to ponder the life which had passed. The skeleton of the once living tumbleweed blew across the land, brushing up against other plants to release seed into the air and across the ground.

As if transported to another place entirely, I began to witness signs of life at every glance. Colors of sage and rust in vast quantities spread across the earth. Dozens of insects darted from certain death on my windshield. Clouds in strange animal shapes danced across the dazzling blue sky. What at first appeared to be an endless monotony of non-descript shrubs suddenly transformed into spiny mounds bejeweled with yellow and pink crowns.

My desert classroom pointed me toward a reality contained not only in the life cycles of plants and animals, but in the cycle of spiritual life as well. When I insist upon my own way, rejecting opportunities divinely prepared to direct me toward the "death" called self-denial, my heart, like an unbroken wheat kernel, remains hard and unfruitful. In dying to my quest for self satisfaction, I can more genuinely comprehend the life I can share with others in the form of a listening ear, a hand to hold, or a cup of water given. Upon closer examination I discover that, like the One who exemplified self-denial, it will only be in a daily death that my life can find its purpose and the hidden signs of His life come into clear focus.

The Elevator

"And the Lord, He is the one who goes before you. He will be with you, He will not leave you or forsake you; do not fear nor be dismayed."

Deuteronomy 31:8 (NKJV)

Standing on the small dock in Southern Oregon overlooking one of the most dangerous sections of the Rogue River, I watched as the rapids pulsed past me, undulating into watery hills and then plunging down into troughs of about four feet—walls of water threatening to drown anything that happened to be unfortunate enough to be caught between them. I found it absolutely ridiculous to have put myself in a position which demanded far more of my fragile mental and emotional capacity than I could afford to expend. The long and agonizing journey of watching my husband slip from vitality and life into the final stages of leukemia had left me far more breakable than I realized. Although I was convinced of his eternal state, and trusting implicitly that he now rested in the presence of God, the three-and-a-half year battle had diverted most of my energy and attention from any self-care to the constant responsibility of attending to the emotional and physical well-being of my husband and children—and the even more constant effort to keep a positive outlook.

Being gently encouraged by some friends to accompany them on our church's annual summer rafting trip on the Rogue River, I was inwardly resistant, but found myself agreeing to join the adventure. The first two hours proved to be more enjoyable than I had hoped as our raft floated along happily over the class I and II rapids. The more than occasional splash of icy water was refreshing enough, but I was glad to be inside the sanctuary of our raft and not in the cold uncertainty of the water. As we progressed down the river, however, the water gained speed dropping low over giant boulders in its path then hurling us forward onto the next section of churning rapids. Our navigator, positioned at the rear of our little island of safety, acted as the rudder, digging his paddle deep into the water to help steer us around the most turbulent areas. His commands to his novice crew were at times nearly drowned out by the ferocious roar of the current. Barely having time to congratulate ourselves for having successfully navigated the chaotic stretch of river before the next set of rapids appeared, we quickly re-oriented ourselves to synchronize our movements in preparation for the next challenge. Plowing through an especially difficult section, we rounded a ferocious bend and simultaneously breathed a sigh of relief as a dock jutting out from the river's edge came into view. Several other rafts from our group were already safely moored on the tiny landing stage, their occupants cheering us on as we paddled in unison to join them.

The sun, gleaming brightly above, not only warmed my skin, but also my heart. Stepping away from the raft, a new sense of understanding trickled into my conscious thoughts, giving me insight into the invitation to accompany this group: Each had either witnessed or participated with me in the long passage through the cancer. They understood, whereas I did not, that my heart was in need of a change of pace, a respite from the worries of how to navigate the next stage of my journey—single parenthood. Feeling a twinge of my former enthusiasm for life re-surface, I even began to enjoy the fact that I had survived the rapid-ordeal we had just endured. As my muscles began to relax, I leaned back against a rock to continue my appreciation of the sun's warming rays. Moments later I was disturbed to find a shadow move across my location, hiding the sun and its warmth from my face. Opening my eyes I saw not a cloud but the shadow of my pastor hovering over me, a smile across his always-cheerful face. Smiling in return, I was tempted to shift my position and renew my siesta, but instead heard his words directing me to follow him over to the dock. Not wanting to appear uninterested (although I was), I dutifully followed him to the edge of the dock where he stood, silently peering out into the section of the river known as The Elevator.

Following his gaze out into the deeper region, I thought I spotted something violently bobbing up and down in that very section of water. Straining against the glare, my eyes confirmed what my brain had been struggling to comprehend, "Why would anyone in their right mind be in this part of the river?" Not only was there one person in the water, there were several, and they were from our group. My teeth began to chatter in unison with my shaking body. As a young girl I had several close encounters in the waters of the Pacific Ocean, and the memory of the fear it produced in me sent an immediate signal to my body and brain: "RUN!" Knowing my pastor had now turned his attention to me, I closed my eyes, willing my ears not to hear the words aimed in my direction, "I think you need to do this, Daryl. It will be good for you to be challenged. Trust me, and just do it!"

If I had had a stick in my hand I might have used it on that dear man. Hadn't I just done what he announced would be for my own good? Hadn't I put myself at risk in the raft as we fought our way through the deep and brutal waters for the past three hours? Was he seriously thinking that death was a good challenge for me at this point? It took several minutes before I was mentally able to put down my imaginary stick. If it had been anyone else on the planet making this suggestion I would have laughed them to scorn, but this was my pastor, my friend who had walked me through other deep and brutal waters only months earlier. How could I mistrust this man who had shown me such compassion and hope?

Giving me all the necessary instructions for surviving the ride through the Elevator, he then hurled himself into the river and swam out to meet the challenge head-on. Following serious thoughts of hiking my way back to the car, I prayed, and willed myself to jump into the river.

An interesting thing happens to the mind and heart when we face our fears. Down in the bottom of the troughs of water, where I had to fight the natural response to breathe in (for I would have breathed in water instead of air) I found that God was there. When the waters thrust my head up and I could see the land again I knew He had brought me through. My victory was secure all along, but I had to believe and take that first step into uncertainty. My fear had vanished in the presence of the One who created the very waters that threatened to drown me moments before, and I knew God had brought me here not just for victory, but to change the course of my life.

But now, thus says the Lord, your creator, O Jacob, and He who formed you, O Israel, "Do not fear, for I have redeemed you; I have called you by name; you are Mine! When you pass through the waters, I will be with you; and through the rivers, they shall not overflow you" (Isaiah 43:1 NASB).

Finding Community

Through the pages of history, countless generations of women have gone through the transition of leaving the family unit to begin a new life in the smaller community of two. Whether the new couple begin their lives in a setting far away from their parents, or dwell in a room attached to the parent's home, the symbolism of the bride and groom becoming a couple distinct from their parents is meant to highlight their unique oneness—two identities willing to form an incredible union in order to become something greater than what they were as individuals. In the months preceding my second marriage, thoughts of community took on new meaning for me as I prepared for a trip to Chicago, hoping for an up close and personal look at the Christian community Jason would be living in while he completed his final year of studies.

Becoming a widow at thirty-two, I found myself the single parent of two small children whose lives had been interrupted by the unimaginable. The current question facing me was, "Will we marry before or after the school year ends?" Given the fact my fiancé would be away for a year, every concern was aimed at the blending of our little family with as much love and support as possible. Understanding the situation, our pastor had suggested that it would be a good idea for me to spend several days in the aforementioned community to find a sense of what living there would be like. In my desire to help my children prepare for the transition I accepted the suggestion, trusting it would answer the questions stampeding through my mind.

Arriving in Chicago in the dark of night, we picked up our rental car and drove slowly to our destination: Maggie House, an old brownstone apartment building nestled in one of the older sections of the city which housed a portion of the large community we had come to visit. Checking in with the pastor who had made the arrangements for our room assignments was the next item on our agenda. As I stepped out of the vehicle, a vague reminder of a childhood lesson filtered through my alarmed thoughts: Never judge a book by its cover. Between the homeless man asleep on the bench in the entry way, the stale darkness of the small room and the dozens of peanut butter sandwiches lying exposed on a large tray, warning signals began to fire in rapid succession at my mother's heart. Trying desperately to hang onto the childhood lesson, I willed myself to think positive thoughts as I sat alone in the entryway while my betrothed went down the hall to find the pastor. I am not sure if I had enough composure at that moment to pray, but I do recall the amused smile on his face when he finally reappeared.

Over breakfast the next morning I was informed that Maggie House was soon to be sold, and if we did indeed move to the Windy City we would not have the pleasure of calling it our home. Relief, blowing over me like a gentle breeze, brought a new sense of tranquility; however, I felt I wasn't to let my guard down just yet. A new hotel several blocks from the shore of Lake Michigan had been recently purchased, and was being refurbished with the plan of consolidating all the members of the large Christian community residing in several brownstones like Maggie House into one location. All the details necessary to operate a five hundred person, self-supporting community known for reaching out to meet the grinding needs of the neighborhood would flow with greater efficiency from one central location.

Preparing for our visit to the new hotel later that morning, we were warned that parking on the street could be risky to the car, and it would be prudent to try and park directly in front of the hotel—if one of the four spaces were unoccupied. Circling the block, we eventually found an empty slot and eased our way into it. The street was busy, cars humming along, and Lake Michigan was in sight beyond some trees. Pulling back the large glass doors, the former glory of the once upscale hotel peeked through the debris from the renovations. Dozens of crystal prisms, coated with years of dust, danced in the breeze as we passed through the doors. Still clothed in heavily flocked wall paper and patterned carpets, the main lobby bristled with activity, workmen hammering and cleaning the embossed ceiling tiles characteristic of the 1930's.

Smiling broadly as we approached, the warmth of the people stationed at the front desk was genuine; their faces covered with a contentment I immediately noticed. After taking us on a brief tour of the main areas, we finished in the dining room and were quickly invited to stay for lunch. Sitting across from the woman in charge of

43

hospitality, I determined to glean every piece of information possible. The community, functioning like a well-oiled machine, boasted nine pastors, who, along with their wives cared for a portion of the people which were grouped into families. Each pastor maintained a specific role within the community and within their family group, assuring that everyone had access to spiritual leadership. The businesses run by the community were as diverse as the people: a roofing company, a painting company, graphic design, several bands and musicians, a crisis pregnancy center, a women's shelter and a clothing store. Living with the intention of having all things in common, everyone was enveloped in the support and care of the entire group.

Relaxing the muscles in my previously tense shoulders, I realized that my objections were not with the people or the lifestyle, but with the location: The middle of the inner city. With the exception of South Chicago, this part of town had the highest crime rate in the city. The poverty was clearly visible. The community lived here to be a witness of the hope they had in Jesus. They lived out a daily belief that living in the comfort of suburban Chicago and only going near the reality of human need when it was convenient would be hypocrisy, and it would tarnish their witness to the neighborhood. So they moved in to help shoulder the immense burdens that screamed from every corner. The question was, "Would I?"

Several days later, after attending the community's outreach service and picnic in a nearby park, we sat down at a picnic table to discuss our future plans. Looking into the eyes of the man I loved, my heart trembled with the recognition that I was not prepared to bring my children into this place. It was too unfamiliar, too far from home, too dangerous. I longed to begin our life together, but my mother's heart was fiercely protective, and I held my ground. "I just can't do this," I finally said. "I can't bring the children here. It's too much. I'm sorry." Still tasting the conflict on my tongue, I was taken completely by surprise by the words which now flowed into my soul, "It's okay. You don't have to. I'll marry you and come home on breaks, or we can wait until I finish. It will work out. Trust me."

Through his words I was offered priceless gifts: Love, community and freedom to choose. There was no pressure to make a decision or figure things out; just the assurance that we were being called together, and wherever we lived, we would be in the loving community of God and each other. I was reminded of Christ Jesus, who offered to all mankind the same priceless gifts: Love that would never fail, community within the fellowship of God and His people and the freedom to choose to accept or reject Him. It was a costly experiment for God to create us with freewill, but as my beloved already knew, love and community cannot be forced. They must be free to choose the path they will take. And therein lays their great worth.

Before the plane delivered me home again, I knew my heart had been miraculously changed, and that our little family would begin life together in a hotel in Chicago's Uptown.

The Healing Balm

"Therefore, if anyone is in Christ, he is a new creation; old things have passed away; behold, all things have become new."

2 Corinthians 5:17 (NKJV)

Sweeping me up into his arms and carrying me across the threshold of our honeymoon suite, my heart filled with gratitude that we had finally begun this journey as husband and wife. Loosening his embrace only slightly, he gently set my feet on the floor. I surveyed the room with approval, my eye catching the enormous vase on the table, absolutely packed with dozens of roses: perfect, unblemished, white roses. Keeping our secluded beachfront destination a secret had been no small task, so the sight of the glorious bouquet caught me by surprise. "Who could have possibly sent these?" I blurted out. Noticing the card tucked among the blooms, I reached for it and slowly read the inscription: "Because God makes all things new". Silent tears fell to the floor as the identity of the sender became known to my fragile heart.

***

It is difficult to describe what takes place in the human heart during times of intense suffering and grief. Not surprisingly, if the agony is of a lengthy duration, the affects can manifest themselves in unanticipated ways. During the long battle with cancer, my first husband Gary and I encountered grief and fears of a depth previously unknown to us. The sheer drama of the trips to the monthly doctor appointments, hoping for a good report yet secretly afraid to hear, took a particular toll on my husband's disposition. Over time he grew less and less amiable, and slipped ever so quietly into a deep cavern of despair and anger. His faith in God remained intact, yet he felt cheated by the diagnosis: three and a half to five years to live.

As the months passed and we approached the second year of the uphill fight, the space between us had become a wall of emotional estrangement. While I can honestly say there was love in the house, I would have been hard pressed to provide a narrative of actions that demonstrated it.

Anger gave way to resentment and flurries of rage-filled antagonisms. Not knowing how to cope, I withdrew, and learned to avoid conflict rather than love him through it. Sensing the emotional distance, my husband reacted by pushing me away even further. It was a long, slow descent into darkness and loneliness.

What we choose to do with our pain, whether we allow it to make us better or make us bitter, greatly depends upon our view of who God is, and who we are in light of that. If we believe that God is indifferent to us, that He has no great investment in humanity or in our daily struggles, then we will not be inclined to call out to Him for help in times of great need. If, however, we believe that God created us from love and from a desire to be loved, then we see ourselves with immense value to the Creator and worthy of His attention. It is from this latter belief that I was able to navigate through the intensity of my pain and loneliness. In His incredible kindness, God heard the cry of my heart and infused me with grace sufficient to live each day with significance.

On Christmas Eve, three and a half years following the diagnosis, my husband's health began to decline with alarming speed. By New Years he had been admitted to the hospital, and I entered one of the most distressing journeys of my life. The nightly vigils at the hospital were excruciating as I was forced to watch not only his life slip away, but also the human dignity which God places into the life of every person. Though many books have been written to assist us through the valley of the shadow of death, none can truly prepare the individual for the intimate thoughts and sadness that prevail as one's loved one marches toward death's door. It is personal and devastating—and yet, for the heart that trusts in God, there is a mysterious triumph in the midst of the unfolding drama.

In the final days of my husband's life our triumph came in the form of an emotional healing between us. The recognition of standing at eternity's door was overpowering, but there was a Presence that stood with us, invading our hearts with peace and the assurance that the transformation from death to life was near. The grief and fears that had once plagued us had been replaced with the blessed promise of standing new and complete in God's presence.

***

Turning my teary eyes toward my new husband, Jason, I pulled him closer in a thankful embrace. The roses and card brought new insight, and I now understood that he had known of my suffering, but viewed it from a distance. Without my knowledge he had silently grieved over my loss. With understanding only given him through the Master's love for me, he now tenderly applied a healing balm to the desire of my broken heart.

The joy of being received as a bride by a husband is a true gift; I had lost the sense of this precious gift through the painful years of my first marriage. And now, crossing the threshold of this new life, I was being welcomed into my husband's heart as a true bride—a new and unblemished creation by God's own doing!

Beauty from the Ashes

"Now all things are of God, who has reconciled us to Himself through Jesus Christ, and has given us the ministry of reconciliation."

2 Corinthians 5:18 (NKJV)

An ocean of men encircled the small table in the center, adorned with candles, bread and chalices. Six women knelt silently before the table, humbled by the acceptance they found in the room. Tears fell silently as familiar hymns rose up from our brothers like waves of peace washing over us.

We gathered at this mountain retreat to find unity and spiritual insight through prayer, but the final evening of our four day prayer journey arrived all too soon. This particular group of pastors had the history of meeting together for the past twelve years to pray; however, this was the first time women ministers had received an invitation to join them. The hope in finding reconciliation between genders as we worshiped and prayed together was visible in the earnest expressions worn on each face.

The previous evening brought the daunting request for the women to serve communion to the men as a balm to the painful wounds between the genders. In the few hours following the invitation, we gathered to pray and discern what our role was to be. As women, most of us were painfully familiar with the wounds of separation between the genders, some which left scars upon our hearts and some which left scars more visible. None of us were prepared for the path this journey was about to take.

As the fire roared in the fireplace of the little meeting room, the Holy Spirit seemed to match the intensity with flames of His own conviction. There was to be no effort on our part to help the men understand the scars we bore. This Communion supper was to bear the marks of repentance by us for the sins women had committed against men: Misuse of our feminine allure. Sins a mother commits toward her son. Pain inflicted by wives upon their husbands. We would represent the masses of women who, consciously or not, left wounds upon the men in their lives, some of which were incurable.

The hymns faded softly into silence, signaling the appointed time for the journey into reconciliation to begin. One by one we began to offer up prayers of confession and repentance on behalf of wives, of mothers, of women. Shaky voices turned to sobbing cries, purging the heart of sins hidden through the years. The weight of our sorrow came from somewhere beyond the room, as if the guilt-cries of women from centuries past had finally found a place to mourn. As the minutes passed, the weight lifted and again the peace returned to settle upon us.

Before we could raise ourselves from our knees, we felt hands being gently laid upon our shoulders and heads. Startled by the touch, I opened my eyes to a scene I will not soon forget: The men had gathered around us, some with hands raised up to the Lord, and others with heads bowed, tears dripping from their cheeks. Our confessions had an unintended effect upon the hearts of these brothers. From somewhere in their masculine minds came the need to comfort us and to fix what seemed quite broken to them. The offering of prayers on our behalf was heartfelt and tender, covering everything from forgiveness and comfort to the lifting of our burdens.

The inevitable transition of focus from us to the men pressed on our hearts. One by one we rose from our knees, and quietly reached for the plates of communion bread on the table. We broke into three stations around the room, putting distance between ourselves for the sake of privacy. The invitation to come and receive was made, ushering in one of the most amazing experiences of my life.

As the men came to receive communion, it was our turn to offer up prayers for them. It only took moments before we realized that when one brother would leave a station, he would merge into the line for the next duo of challis bearing women, as if something compelled him to seek another blessing, receive another washing from the bread and cup. Tears continued to roll from faces, bearing witness of the cleansing taking place within.

His shoulders slumped forward, refusing to show forth the full stature of the man now standing before me. Placing my hand on his shoulder I began to pray, words barely escaping my mouth before this bear of a man was reduced to a sobbing, grieving boy. "She said she could never love me. I've never heard my mother say, "I love you." His head buried into my shoulder, the sobs pulsed through him as the little boy finally faced the giant he had locked away in his heart years ago.

Every mothering instinct within me seemed to move into emergency mode as I tried to comprehend the magnitude of my brother's pain and suffering over his lifetime. I noticed that I was gently rocking him now though his cries had not yet subsided. "Every mother loves her children," I whispered to him. "She may not know how to show it due to choices she made which may have imprisoned her emotions; but nevertheless, she still loves her children. Your mother loves you, even if she has never said it." The groan that rose up from his heart spilled out, sending him into another wave of sobs more violent than before. There was nothing I could do now but hold him, and let the weight of his burden roll from his heart onto the shoulders of Another, the One who would carry this burden from now on.

In an email a few weeks later I learned that through this journey into reconciliation my brother found the strength and healing to care for his mother in a new way. No longer plagued by fears that he was unlovable, he was free to love her just as she was—no longer needing a sign of her love to validate his worth as a son. The remains of his shattered heart had been carefully gathered by the One who lovingly transformed it into a heart that resembled His own.

Pride and Prejudice

"My brethren, do not hold your faith in our glorious Lord Jesus Christ with an attitude of personal favoritism."

James 2:1 (NASB)

"Lady, you're on the edge of trouble!" announced the security guard as he stared down at me. Standing just inside the door of the health clinic nestled among the dreary urban surroundings, I found myself clutching my five year old daughter's hand even tighter. I sensed by his tone of voice and the intensity of his eyes that he was issuing a warning, and I was taking him seriously.

Earlier that morning, we had begun the routine adventure of arriving on time for a doctor's appointment at a free clinic on the Near North side of Chicago. This may not seem a troublesome matter to some, however, learning to rely on others for every single need was a new experience for us. Accepting the transportation freely offered through Jesus People USA* was a step further into the fringes of my comfort zone.

Living in "community" ushers you directly into the arena of "all things in common," including the use of the Deacon of the Day who was responsible to safely deliver all who had appointments to and from their destinations. Being the last in the common vehicle to be dropped at our appointment meant we would be the last to be retrieved. Hours later with no trace of the Deacon on the horizon, I brushed aside the veneer of "whatever happens is cool" and began to conjure up a plan to return us to the safety of our sixth floor rooms back at the Chelsea Hotel.

The "L" Train, Chicago's famous elevated train system, had a stop at either end of this particular section of town, and I imagined Casey and I could easily walk to either one. Bravely, I bundled up my little one, and walked through the clinic doors, ready to embrace the next adventure. Contemplating the risks and realities of living in the inner city once we were outside, my composure quickly vanished. Believing strongly that coming to Chicago while my husband finished seminary was all part of God's plan for us, I knelt down on the sidewalk in front of the clinic, grabbed my daughter's hand and prayed for God to protect us as we walked.

Silently, I decided that I would keep my eyes straight ahead, minding my own business. "It's safer to keep to oneself," I mumbled under my breath, and cautiously took the first steps around the corner into the unknown. Not more than a minute passed before a man on the opposite side of the street, drinking from a brown paper bag, stepped out into the street intersecting his path with ours. I determined not to say a word nor even look his direction when, to my complete amazement, I found myself blurting out, "Hello, how are you?" Feeling my heart pound inside my chest, I waited for the inevitable response. "Hi," was all he said, as he continued walking on ahead of us.

Wiping the sweat from my forehead, I relaxed a little and mutely thanked God for the quiet encounter. Looking up the street to the corner, I had a vague feeling that I had seen the massive apartment complex which lay in our path somewhere before. As we drew nearer to the sign announcing the name of this enormous community, I noticed that there was no grass in the play areas, only dirt. Many apartments had no screens on the windows, and laundry was hanging from many of those same windows. Everything, from the buildings to the ground, was the same shade of grey-brown, shrouding this place in a veil of hopelessness. Lowering my eyes to the green metal letters on the fence, I read "Cabrini Green," and that's when it hit me. Cabrini Green had begun back in the 1940's as an experimental public housing project. The need for inexpensive housing was so great that it had grown to over 15,000 residents at its height. Over the years the name Cabrini Green had become well known for gang violence and neglect. Squeezing Casey's hand again, I quickened our pace, trying to put distance between this place and us.

Turning the corner, I peered ahead to the last stretch of sidewalk that lay between the L stop and our current location, and at that same moment my heart froze. Only a few yards before us stood the same man whom I had unwillingly greeted moments before. He appeared to be in a serious conversation with another man, who glanced up at us periodically. It was no stretch of the imagination to realize they were watching us, possibly planning something. There was no way to avoid this roadblock, and dashing across the busy street with a five-year-old simply wasn't an option. Shooting another silent prayer up to God, I braced myself, trying not to alarm my daughter, and continued walking toward the men.

My fear became reality as we approached them. Turning directly to me, the first man said, "Ma'am, do you have a token for the L Train you could give me?" My mind scrambled to recall what I had in my small purse. Realizing I had only one token, which I would need to return home, I searched for a safe answer. "I don't have one to give you, but I do have a dollar," I managed. Affirming that this would be just fine, he reached for the dollar. "God bless you," he said, looking me directly in the eyes, then turned and walked away.

I have searched my heart many times since that afternoon on the streets of Chicago wondering where the seeds of racism had first begun to sprout in my mind. Would I have felt the same level of anxiety if this man had my skin color? Perhaps if I were walking along the streets in the safer or the nicer part of town, our stroll would have been merry rather than worrisome. Shame, rising from my heart and turning my otherwise pale complexion crimson, I lifted yet another prayer up to God, this time asking His forgiveness.

Jesus People USA is a Christian intentional community which resides in Uptown on the north side of the city of Chicago, IL. Founded in 1972, it is the largest of the remaining communities from the Jesus Movement. JPUSA joined the Evangelical Covenant Church as a member congregation in 1989.

Well, That's Deep!

"I waited patiently for the Lord; and He inclined to me, and heard my cry. He also brought me up out of a horrible pit, out of the miry clay, and set my feet upon a rock, and established my steps."

Psalm 40:1-2 (NKJV)

Brilliant blue crowded every inch of the summer sky and overpowered the melancholic feel of the inner city. Staring upward for the last time at the old hotel that had been our home and place of refuge, we squeezed into our small car and breathed a sigh of relief. Sharing the back seat with our two children was Archimedes, the hamster they had recently been given and were not about to relinquish. Fresh from seminary and content to complete the eight-month experience of living communally in Chicago's Uptown, our little family gratefully accepted the more than generous offer to rent an old farm house situated on five blissfully quiet acres on the northern edge of Hillsboro, Oregon. We were coming home—home to my husband's roots, and my home since the mid 1980's. Becoming a blended family within the last nine months, the country-like atmosphere of our new surroundings would fit perfectly into my plan to nurture us into a healthy, happy unit. With ample open space there would be room to run freely, explore the old barns, and even plant a vegetable garden. Though I knew little about the rhythms of country living, I was willing to learn and eager to move into our new sanctuary, free from the noise and dangers of the inner city.

Growing up in the comfort of middle class America, I took for granted two very essential elements crucial to one's health and comfort: water and heat. The farm drew its supply of water from an old well, and as is common on the periphery of Oregon city life, our heat was supplied through the hundred gallon oil tank just outside the back door and an old wood stove uniquely situated in the upstairs bathroom. Our landlord Beth, a wonderful, generous woman who had raised her children and then buried her husband all while calling this farm home, instructed us in the proper use of both well and oil tank. Anticipating a wonderful adventure out on the farm, I brushed aside the red flags that waved along the fringes of my thoughts after she informed us, "The well is temperamental, and occasionally loses pressure—but don't worry, all you need to do is keep a daily eye on the pump."

Surviving from June until October without incident, our confidence grew as we neared the winter months and cozy nights bundled under the multitude of quilts left for our use. The daytime temperatures quickly turned crisp, and the nights were just plain cold. As the winds whipped across the open fields surrounding the house, we began to notice how many of the old window frames had been jimmied with folded newspaper in an effort to keep the winds from blowing through the house instead of around it. Needing to heat the house at higher temperatures as the weeks slipped past, the calendar flipped to November and it was soon time to begin Thanksgiving preparations. Spending less time outside during the colder days, and ignoring the old adage, "Out of sight, out of mind", my daily ritual of checking well and oil tank evolved into a weekly one.

Making a dash from the warm comfort of our quilt to the thermostat on an uncomfortably cold morning, I gave it a crank, and raced back to bed to wait for the house to heat up enough to bear standing in the kitchen while making breakfast. Dosing off for several minutes, I was jolted from my morning catnap with the sounds of the kids complaining, "Mom…Mom…Mommy! I'm freeeeezing!" Always the vigilant mother, I woke my husband and sent him out to investigate why the house was still so cold. Returning with a long stick in his hand several minutes later, he wearily informed me that it was quite impossible to heat a house, especially an old, drafty farm house, without oil. Not amused in the least, I made the frigid trek from bed to closet and quickly layered jeans and sweatshirts over thermal underwear. By mid-morning I humbly phoned my mom who lived within the city limits, and whose house warmed quite efficiently with her natural gas furnace, and accepted her invitation to stay until Monday—when the oil company resumed its deliveries.

Learning several lessons following the oil crisis, I made a mental list: Never, under any circumstances, put an empty aerosol can into a metal burn barrel and proceed to burn the trash. Keeping an eye on the water pressure gauge is far easier than priming the pump. Swinging too high and for too long on the old tire swing really does bring the morning's breakfast to light. Finally, mice can make their home just as snug in the dashboard of your car as they can under a rock pile.

As springtime arrived with brisk winds and grey skies, we noticed that we had to prime the pump to the well with increasing regularity. One warm morning my father-in-law, ever the fix-it man, and my mother-in-law, ever the optimist, planned to spend the day with us tackling the larger jobs like pruning apple trees and investigating the problem with the water pump. With my brother-in-law following close behind, we each set out to make a dent in the workload.

To this day, it isn't clear to me just how I managed to end up being the gopher for everyone else that morning, but gopher I was, and while re-tracing my steps up the side porch for the umpteenth time I heard the panicked cries of my father-in-law coming from the direction of the back deck, adjacent to the well. Rounding the corner of the house, I saw the large iron disc used for covering the well pushed aside, and the green garden hose tied to the trunk of a birch tree; the remaining length made a path directly into the mouth of the well then disappeared into its depths. With no one else in sight, I ran to the mouth, peering into the watery pit. About ten feet from the rim of the well was my father-in-law, hanging precariously above the water line a good twenty feet below him, the garden hose tied around his waist. "I'm stuck!" he shouted. "Get help—get it quick! I'm slipping!"

Trying to shout for help, I found my voice stifled with panic. Having insufficient strength to pull him out of the well myself, there was nothing left to do but run for it and find the rest of the crew in order to attempt a mass rescue. Dashing past the garage and across the yard, I found no one in sight. I hurried to the barn and then out to the oak grove—still no signs of family hard at work. Turning around, I ran as fast as I could toward the house, my heart nearly pounding out of my chest. Reaching the well, I cried out pitifully, "Dale, everyone is gone! I don't know what to do!"

The phrase pregnant pause brings all sorts of things to mind, but in that moment, as Dale hesitated ever so slightly, my eyes caught sight of several shadows approaching from behind me. Suspicion, rising from the well of my gullible heart and flooding my mind, sent me reeling on my heels to see what cast the shadowy figures across the well. Broad smiles were plastered across the faces of the guilty parties, confirming my doubts. Looking back into the well, my father-in-law still hanging suspended and sporting a mischievous smile, pulled himself up by the garden hose and climbed out of the well. As the realization hit that I had fallen prey to the collective humor of my husband's family, I began to chuckle, sweat pouring from my blushing face. In the aftermath of my dismay, my emotions quieted sufficiently in time to enjoy our family lunch on the tree-lined deck.

From the archives of our family history the incident at the well has become legend. At the time, I promised to return in like fashion some form of good humored retaliation. Although I regret I was unable to out-wit Dale before He entered Heaven's gates, on several occasions I came close. From my uninformed vantage point those many years ago, I saw someone I loved helplessly stuck in a pit. In my alarm I tried to do everything humanly possible to save him, but my efforts simply weren't sufficient. My cries fell on deaf ears, and my panic could not produce a single witness to share my burden.

Though Dale faced no real threat as he hung suspended in the well, many people today find their lives have indeed become nothing less than a horrible pit. At times the discouragements we face can feel as if we are being sucked into the suffocating mire of impossible circumstances. Is there no one to hear our cries? No one who will rescue us from the deep well of our burdens?

Truly, our efforts can be valiant at times. Our desire to rescue others from their pain or struggle is notable; however, when we come right down to it, all our blood, sweat and tears will never be enough to pull someone out from the horrible pit of eternal separation from God. It is the gift of un-repayable grace, offered freely and without reservation by the One who peers into the dark abyss of our failures and sin, and without panic offers us the only sufficient way of escape through His own Son.

Thirsty

"My soul thirsts for God, for the living God."

Psalm 42:2 (NIV)

The assignment was simple: Spend an hour alone with God and just listen; however, in spite of my current location along beautiful Ecola Creek, a small, Oregon tributary which feeds into the magnificent Pacific Ocean, my heart remained burdened. My soul felt as parched as the cracked ground of a dry riverbed in mid-summer. Nothing seemed to relieve my dilemma; even my attempts to sing uplifting songs of praise faded into the breeze like a vapor. The creek was bubbling along in apparent opposition to my present condition, and I found even this to be annoying. What was to be a time of reflection and prayer had become a series of taunts from nature, as though it were defying me to find something comforting in my surroundings.

Seagulls flew low overhead, their haunting calls sounding hollow against the distant roar of the surf. Butterflies touched down lightly on the wildflowers behind the sandbanks. With beauty enveloping me on every side, it oddly produced only weariness inside. Stopping next to the edge of the creek, a fragment of a verse from the Psalms blew across the surface of my mind, "...in a dry and thirsty land where there is no water."(Psalm 63:1 NKJV) Though I chuckled to myself, I couldn't help but note the irony of this particular verse making its way into my thoughts.

Tossing the words over and over, they gradually evolved into a prayer. "Father, I'm so thirsty. I have nothing to give. My soul is empty and dry. I can't find my way out of this place without Your Spirit. Please lead me." Staring blankly at the rippling current, something caught the corner of my eye. Looking up, I found the sky empty except for some clouds off in the distance. Returning my gaze to the water, I closed my eyes and listened instead.

I don't remember what caught me more by surprise, the fact that I now heard something I hadn't before, or that the sound was strangely close to my ear. I quickly opened my eyes—nothing. My first thought was that my current state of mind had now given way to imaginations. Or perhaps this was further ridicule from nature. Before I could mull over my ingrown thinking any further the noise returned; faint, yet a bit like the gentle flapping of a flag in the breeze. Turning to bring the source into view, I was startled to see only inches above my head a brown and white bird, perhaps about eight inches long, hovering directly above me. Remaining suspended in the air for about ten seconds with its eyes fixed upon me, it darted away just as quickly as it had appeared.

Contemplating what had just taken place, a gentle impression came into view. I had admitted to God that without the aid of His Spirit I could not navigate through the parched wilderness of my heart, and in answer to my prayer He had sent a representative of His Spirit to assure me that my request had been heard in the King's throne room. As His Spirit had once hovered over His Son long ago, He now tenderly sent this messenger to remind me His power and grace were available to me as well.

An Open Door

"I am the door; if anyone enters through Me, he shall be saved, and shall go in and out, and find pasture."

John 10:9 (NASB)

Finally scraping together enough money to purchase a home of our own, we exchanged the spacious and tranquil farm house for a 1915 barn-turned-house situated in the heart of downtown Hillsboro—an historic but quickly growing section of the Portland Metro area. Reflecting on our experiences living in the multi-cultural inner-city of Chicago two years earlier, we had returned to Oregon with a completely revised perspective concerning the boundaries we commonly erect in an effort to feel secure. Unable to rival Chicago's ethnic diversity, however, Hillsboro shared some of the Windy City's challenges in blending culture with respect for one another. As parents, we desired the melting-pot approach of exposing our children to many differing points of view, traditions and even cuisine. Relishing in the opportunity to put down roots, our new home was at the cross-roads of several different ethnic and economic arenas, the perfect setting to help us and our children continue embracing other cultures.

Immersing myself in the largely joyous adventure referred to as home school, the transition from mom to teacher each morning was occasionally met with whining; until the children learned I was more than serious about successfully educating them. Nurturing a love for learning in the roomy fields surrounding the city, where tree frogs and barn owls delight young hearts, I had not anticipated how our kids might feel observing their peers walking home from school laughing and sharing life. At the end of the school year I realized the inevitable transition to public school was looming large on the horizon.

As the warm summer days passed leisurely by, the kids joined ranks and began a campaign to break down my resistance to enrolling them in our local public elementary school. With a bit of reservation about giving up the time we spent together each week day, I agreed to schedule a visit with the principal to discuss the options for educating our children. To my surprise and delight he confided that if he weren't an educator in the public school system himself, he would opt to do what we had just agreed upon: home school our children until lunch time with a focus on science, art and music, and let the school instruct them in math and reading in the afternoon. I was happy with the plan as both Sean and Casey had learned to read at an early age, and devouring a good book was high on their list of life's little pleasures. Never truly interested in math beyond fractions, I gladly passed the baton over to the professional educators. Pleased with the results by the end of the school year, we agreed to let them participate full time when they returned again in the fall.

In preparation for the upcoming change in routine, I began thinking about how to fill the empty hours awaiting me in the not too distant future. Interested in furthering my skills in conversational Spanish, I considered enrolling in some classes at the local Hispanic Cultural Center, but a glance at our finances ruled out that option. Persistent in desire to reach out to our Spanish speaking neighbors, I began to pray, asking God to bring someone to me with whom I could share an English-Spanish speaking friendship. Several weeks later, while sitting at the kitchen table reviewing the morning's rush to get everyone out the door on time, God answered my request.

Startled by the forceful knock on my front door, I hurried to answer, tripping over the rug in the entry way. To say I was surprised to find a Hispanic woman staring up at me is an understatement, but her words caught me completely off guard: "Hi. I'm Maria. Can I come in?" As I welcomed her into my home, I remembered my earlier appeal for a new friendship. This was God's special answer, hand-picked and eager to plunge ahead without a second thought— and I wasn't about to drop the ball.

Spending time together often, Maria brought me bulbs and plantings from her garden, and I fed her lunch or listened to her stories about distant family memories. Months into our friendship, I accepted her peculiarities as part of her culture, and didn't pay much attention to them until one afternoon when I received a phone call from her daughter. Sitting down to absorb what I was hearing, I learned that Maria's oddities went far deeper than I suspected. With somber tenderness, her daughter informed me that her mother had been diagnosed with bi-polar disorder several years earlier, and in recent weeks had refused to take her medication. Acting unpredictably and erratically, most days she forgot to eat anything at all. Without her medication she was at risk, and her daughter had called to ask for my help—she wanted me to testify at an upcoming committal hearing in order to have Maria taken into custody within the mental health system. With each of her explanations, I connected the fragments of my friend's behavior as though I were putting together a very large puzzle. She was floundering in the labyrinth of her own mind, and I knew in my heart it was in Maria's best interest for me to honor her daughter's request. Her committal hearing was the last time I saw Maria as she refused to see me when I came to visit her in the hospital—in her mind I had betrayed her, and this was unforgivable.

It has been many years since I first met Maria on my front porch, but I sometimes think of her and wonder what path her life took following that fateful court hearing. I've grown accustomed to God answering prayers in incredibly specific ways, undeniable evidence that He listens and responds as we take the time to pray in ways that make room for Him to do something beyond our limitations. Perhaps the most important lesson I received from this special friend-of-my-past is that God works with intentional purpose when He sends people into our lives. Sometimes they arrive at our request, other times at His. He is constantly seeking someone to open the door of their heart and invite whomever He has placed on the other side into a relationship. It may involve more time than we feel we are able to spend. It may require we lay down our prejudices and embrace someone labeled peculiar in the eyes of the world. Most definitely it will require that we imitate the invitation and grace-filled offer God made available to the church in Laodicea: "Behold, I stand at the door and knock. If anyone hears My voice and opens the door, I will come in to him and dine with him, and he with Me." (Revelation 3:20 NKJV) As we open the door so that others may hear His invitation, He enters too, broadening our capacity to love. Through the portal of human relationship, God extends His compassion, awakening our need for something more significant than our own self-existence.

A Break in My Heart

"For My thoughts are not your thoughts, neither are your ways My ways,"
declares the Lord. "As the heavens are higher than the earth, so are My ways
higher than your ways, and My thoughts than your thoughts."

Isaiah 55:8-9 (NIV)

Biting my lip to keep the tears from spilling over, I forced my hands to join the celebratory applause. My dear friends had just announced their joyful news: A new life, another child, a prayer answered! The bitterness of my own unfulfilled desires coated my tongue; every tendon within me fought to restrain my impulse to run from the sanctuary as fast as possible. Forcing my sorrow and shame to return to the depths of my heart, I picked up the morning's song sheet and pretended to worship.

Several hours later in the shelter of my bedroom, I sank to my knees to question the One who alone gives life. I found my ability to rebel against the joy of my friend quite shocking, and I buried my face in the plump down comforter and let the tears flow freely. "I'm so tired Lord. What kind of person am I that cannot enter into the joy of my friend? If this desire to have another child causes me to digress to such an ugly place, please, just take the desire away—take it away completely." As my tears fell, a strange silence entered my heart, giving way to a new and profound peace. In the stillness of the moment God heard my confession, my plea, and had mercifully replaced desire with contentment.

For nearly seven years following my second marriage I lived with the hope that there would be another child in our little family. And for seven years I witnessed the majority of my thirty-something friends welcome this very news, joyously receiving a new life into their arms. With each New Year's celebration I remained acutely aware that my window of opportunity was closing; although I was physically strong and active, the chances of a healthy pregnancy after the age of forty were significantly reduced. Approaching the fall of my thirty-ninth year, I welcomed this new contentment and resolved to step into the world of diapers and baby bottles with my friend. I would be there for her and take pleasure in the miracle of this new life so lovingly placed within her. There was no sign on the horizon of the coming tempest which would soon engulf my heart.

Working a part time job, raising two adolescents and married to a pastor, I brushed aside the "little female annoyances" that began poking at the periphery of my thoughts. When the calendar flipped to November and the approach of our seventh anniversary came into view I couldn't ignore the warning signs any longer. I let down my guard, purchased the little package with the tell-tale test-strip, and took the bull by the horns. The next morning I sat in total disbelief while staring at the positive results of the pregnancy test. Knowing there was room for error in these over-the-counter kits, I drove to the pharmacy later that evening to purchase another. Being armed with twice the ammunition and assuring myself this was just a fluke,

I allowed a slight chuckle to escape from my lips, and pulled the covers up around my neck.

Actively living out my belief in God for many years, I must admit that I was facing a serious crisis of faith. I had not so much as flinched with hesitation from the day God removed all desire to have another child from me—until the following morning. Disbelief surrounded me as I read the positive result of the second test-strip. I fought to stifle the force of doubt quickly rising within. "Can this really be? After all these years I'm pregnant? Will this little one inside of me be at risk because of my age?" While the questions continued to massage my doubts, I steadied myself and went to unveil the news to my husband. Taking the news with greater faith and grace than I had, he hugged me tightly with joy, and assured me all would be well. God would lead us through this chapter of our lives as He had through all the previous ones.

At my calculations I was approximately five weeks along as preparations were being made for our family Thanksgiving celebration. Allowing my emotions to roam unshielded in joy, I optimistically entered into the mysterious awe of knowing a life was again growing within me. Deciding to postpone sharing our wonderful secret until the New Year mainly because of the risk of an early first term miscarriage, I took delight in thoughts of contributing to the merriment of Christmas with our long-awaited news. As the days slipped by and the leaves made their final journey to the ground in mid-December, the first winds of the approaching storm began to blow, bringing with them the chill and darkness of uncharted waters.

It was normal, the doctors said, for a woman of my age to have some slight bleeding during pregnancy. There was no cause for concern unless the bleeding increased or I experienced sustained cramping. When the cramps began a few days later I found myself pushed along by waves of uneasiness, afraid to give in to what I sensed was the end of a dream. I clung to a distant hope, trying to keep it afloat. On New Year's Eve, while my husband struggled to stay awake in the distressing moments of my terror, the final surge of death and sorrow crashed around me like a tempest.

I am challenged to describe the final hours before the tiny life I carried was swept away from my body. It was close to midnight, and the radio station was still playing Christmas carols in the background. As the bleeding intensified and the cramping pounded my abdomen as if I were a pebble on the shore, I tried to awaken my husband to take me to the hospital. He remembers clearly my calls for help, but it was as if he were across some chasm, unable to shake off the fog of sorrow-filled sleep. He mentioned later feeling like one of the disciples in the Garden of Gethsemane, trying to watch with the Lord in His sorrow, but wholly given over to sleep. Perhaps it is the sleep of despair.

I distinctly remember the sense that this was a journey I was to take alone. It was truly a dark night of the soul, a necessary passage from the elementary principles of faith to the rigorous pursuit of all that is real and good about the God Who loves us without condition. Lying still between the rounds of fatal cramps, my thoughts were impressed with a certain passage of Scripture. Almost instinctively, I clung to hope as though God had thrown a life preserver into the raging swells that threatened to drown me. Unknown to me at the time, I was indeed being given words leading to life, but not in the manner I was hoping for: "Ask and it will be given to you; seek and you will find; knock and the door will be opened to you. For everyone who asks receives; he who seeks finds; and to him who knocks, the door will be opened. Which of you, if his son asks for bread, will give him a stone?" (Matthew7:7-9 NIV) Hadn't I been asking for the life of this child? Hadn't I been seeking God's help in this dark hour? Truly I was knocking hard upon the door of God's heart as the hours passed by. There was confidence that this was God's word to me—all would be well. God was listening.

Breathing a sigh of relief as the pulsing in my womb momentarily subsided, I lay in the stillness listening to the faint carol in the background. "Be near me Lord Jesus, I ask Thee to stay, close by me forever and love me I pray. Bless all the dear children in Thy tender care, and take us to heaven to live with Thee there." As the tears fell like hot wax across my face, soaking my neck, my hair, and the pillow, the error in my interpretation of the Scripture passage began to burn more fiercely than the waves of pain. The reality of it took my breath away and I broke into sobs as the final surge gained momentum to forever strip away this child from my arms. God was indeed answering my prayer, but in His Sovereignty had chosen to answer by bringing His child home into His arms, not mine. To be loved and nurtured in His Presence, not mine. It would be some time before I could realize that I wasn't being given an enormous stone.

It is incredibly difficult for the human heart and mind to step outside of emotion and reason to walk into the arena of faith; a faith which demands a daily battle to believe that God is good in spite of the circumstances. While we tend to lurk on the edges of that happy faith that speaks of bright futures, happiness and clear understanding, there comes the day when God asks of us, "Will you trust Me even if I hide My face from you? Will you trust My heart when you have no logical reason to do so?" I've come to recognize this request by God not as a place of despair, but a beckoning into the fellowship of His sufferings—the hidden place close to the heart of God that asks, "Will you watch with Me for this hour, this moment? Will you step over the safety of simple faith into the borders of My suffering for the sin of the world?"

In the days following our little one's entrance into her Creator's arms, I came to that place most of us will come to one day: the hour when we simply need to ask God "Why?" Although it may be considered weakness or doubt by some to ask Almighty God why He has allowed such sorrow into our lives, I believe there are times when God, in His compassion, answers those questions; and this He did for me. Staring at the ceiling as I numbly lay on the couch during the first days of my fractured dreams, I found the right hour to lay my "Why" before the Throne of Grace—and in His mercy He answered:

"You have a position of leadership in My church, and with that comes the responsibility of understanding how raw the human experience can be. If you cannot understand their despair, how will you comfort or lead them? From this moment on we are going to take a long, hard look at humanity—the depths of sin and its consequences, and why I had to die because of it."

There was no sense of discipline with these words placed upon my heart, but rather the assurance that in His sovereign purposes God had chosen to lead me through experiences shared by millions of souls who grieve and bleed just as I do. Yes, the path has been severe, the furnace blistering; but I've come through with the understanding that God's ways involve much more than I can understand, and I am comforted by the knowledge that one day, not in my time but in His, I will see my child for the first time and this break in my heart will finally be mended.

T L F

"They did not receive the things promised; they only saw them and welcomed them from a distance. And they admitted that they were aliens and strangers on earth."

Hebrews 11:13 (NIV)

Acronyms. Word substitutes recognizable as a series of letters which are only understood by those who have been taught their meaning. In former years some of the better known acronyms were: PDQ: Pretty darn quick! SOS: Save our ship! Or, ASAP: As soon as possible. Thanks to the "text generation" there is a resurrection of acronyms intended to save time while texting. LOL: Laugh out loud! OMG: Oh my gosh! BFF: Best friends forever! You get the picture.

With little need for acronyms in my life apart from the occasional RSVP at the end of an invitation, I said my tearful goodbyes to family and friends and followed my husband, freshly commissioned as an officer in the United States Air Force, into the military way of life. Hello acronyms—goodbye rich and meaningful communication! Unwillingly ushered into this new form of communication within minutes of arriving at our first duty assignment, we drove into the parking lot of what was to be our home for the next two weeks. Fixing my eyes onto the unwelcoming brown letters painted across the side of our dwelling, I read: TLF.

Had I been taught their meaning prior to our arrival, I might have turned the car around then and there.

Living almost my entire childhood in the same house, I found the words Temporary Lodging Facility to be sterile and unfriendly. After all, a house is not a "lodging facility," it's a home; a place where you can find sanctuary, be yourself, and escape the hustle of the day in the comfort and company of your family. How could someone reduce the meaning of "home" to "facility," and a momentary one at that? Despite my skepticism, I stood at the threshold of a journey which I sensed was certain to instruct me in new ways. The difficulty was not in the fact that I felt more than a little displaced, but rather in attempting to remain supportive of my husband's new career while my senses assaulted my thoughts. My formerly civilian-trained eyes quickly transformed to uncover, with military precision, any and all evidence of previous occupation in this government-issued lodging facility.

Our apartment was standard issue: a living room with sofa, recliner, coffee table and television. The bedrooms and bathrooms included all the basic items needed to keep one's self clean and rested. Various cleaning aids, resting in a small plastic bowl on the kitchen counter, fit neatly under the Xeroxed sign covered in plastic and taped to the wall. On it were the regulations for staying in our temporary lodging facility, along with all the necessary phone numbers we might need to help us navigate our way through all the acronyms, which replaced real names in real offices around the air base. Nestled between the edge of the cupboard and the refrigerator was a Pandora's Box of plastic grocery bags waiting for re-use. When called into service, the frayed edges on the broom reminded me that someone else, perhaps just as uncertain as I, had swept this same floor, praying for the secrets of adjustment to this new life.

Hidden behind the cupboard doors lurked several leftovers from the previous tenants. From the half empty salt and pepper shakers decorated with brightly colored vegetables to envelopes of instant oatmeal came further confirmation that we were not the first to arrive, and we would certainly not be the last to occupy this dwelling. We were merely passing through. From now on home would be wherever the Air Force sent us; we had become sojourners.

Trying to digest that thought, I let my mind wander back in time and rest on the story of another sojourner: Abraham. Asked to leave his homeland too, he set out for a new land that would be made known to him only upon his arrival. Carrying his tents and all his earthly goods with him, I wonder, did he too feel displaced and uncertain?

While pondering this ancient patriarch making his trek across the terrain of what is now Iraq with relatives and camels in tow, something familiar, yet distant made its way into my thoughts. It is human to desire roots—tangible evidence of our secure place in this world; a certain stability through the years which leaves a mark on us and gives us a sense of connectedness to those who came before us. The irony of this human desire is that nothing in this life is permanent. Our friends will mature and develop interests other than our childhood games. Our children will grow up and move on. Our homes will eventually break down. And our bodies will age and give out. As much as we long for permanency, the truth is that this life and all we know of it is temporary-quite temporary indeed. We are walking, breathing TLF's!

Before I could meander too far down that particular path of thinking, an inaudible, quiet Voice interrupted my thoughts, "This life is temporary, but you are not." Immediately recognizing the Source of this truth, I came to rest on another fact about the ancient sojourner Abraham and his wife Sarah: "They did not receive the things promised; they only saw them and welcomed them from a distance. And they admitted that they were aliens and strangers on earth. People who say such things show that they are looking for a country of their own. If they had been thinking of the country they had left, they would have had opportunity to return. Instead, they were looking for a better country—a heavenly one. Therefore God is not ashamed to be called their God, for He has prepared a city for them." (Hebrews 11:13-16 NIV)

Smiling at the epiphany, I reflected on the acronym TLF once more. What had once offended now became a revelation, and I am certain God planned it that way.

Rock Solid Clarity

"Be strong and of good courage; do not be afraid, nor be dismayed, for the Lord your God is with you wherever you go."

Joshua 1:9 (NKJV)

The lessons I have learned about life while strolling along the Oregon shoreline are nothing less than remarkable. I suppose the wide open space and the comfort of the rhythmic waves calms my mind and elevates my soul beyond the cacophony of thoughts assailing me during the average day. Approaching the monolithic Haystack Rock in the early hours of the morning, I was in need of some clarity and direction for my life. The tide was unusually low, exposing at least to my eyes, this never before seen portion of the massive rock. With a bit of the west coast pioneering spirit, I took off my shoes and let the near icy water cover my feet. Exhilarated by the cold I pressed on, moving closer to a section of smaller rocks now exposed from beneath their watery garments.

Living my childhood and adolescence near the Pacific Ocean afforded me numerous opportunities to discover marine life along the coast. Spotting starfish had been a fairly common childhood experience for me; however, what I now beheld with wide-eyed wonder were shimmering, star-shaped jewels masquerading as sea creatures! Orange, red, chartreuse and purple hues mingled together forming a tapestry fit for exhibit in a gallery. As the tide washed in to temporarily hide the display, I anticipated with childish delight the next peek at my colorful discovery.

Pausing as the foamy surf receded, I glanced out toward the horizon, scanning for signs of life. What held my gaze was not animal life, but rather the rhythmic approach of the waves tumbling in from the vast sea beyond and crashing against a smaller, jagged rock. Swallowing the rock in a turbulent, churning commotion, I imagined the bubbling brew of a witch's cauldron. Secret fear, threatening to escape the closet of my childhood memories, coerced me sufficiently to send shivers down my back. Vulnerable to the powerful emotion, I stood mesmerized as I entertained my juvenile fear of being consumed by the thunderous hammer of mighty waves.

With the frigid splash of water against my legs jarring me back into the present, I jumped back to avoid getting completely soaked. Lessons from years past pushed their way into the front of my thoughts, reminding me that it is not always wise to hide my fears in the hope that they will vanish away along life's journey. The impression gently urging me to respond, I again turned my eyes to the disturbing image out at sea. "Why is this significant, Lord?" I mused. "How can this troubling image give me clarity?"

In the roar of waves beyond my reach I sensed an invitation to abandon my secure location on the shore and swim out to the very center of the uncontrollable sea. Shivering again as the idea pressed with increasing urgency, I blurted out, "I can't do it, Lord! I can't go out there. I am not a strong swimmer. I will drown!" Still, the appeal remained as did my objections. After several moments of conflicting thoughts a light began to dawn in my soul, and this time the waves brought the calm of an answer instead of the sense of peril: "Do not be afraid to go where I call you, My child. I will be there with you even in the midst of the sea. You will not drown because I will be with you." As revelation came so did tranquility, and I now understood that the picture of the turmoil was an invitation to go into the chaos of people's lives; not because I could save them, but because God was with me and I'd be taking His peace into the midst of their turbulence.

Understanding, washing over me like waves over the sand, compelled me to look up at the top of Haystack, only yards from where I stood. Craning my neck to get a perspective of what was above, my eyes captured a wondrous sight: Seagulls diving off the edge of the cliff, wings held against their bodies, falling straight down as though there was no ground to halt their descent. At a precise moment each bird abruptly spread out his wings, and was effortlessly lifted into flight by invisible air currents. Without strain they sailed smoothly along wherever the wind took them, landing peacefully on the sand below.

Once again life's parables afforded me a glimpse into the Heavenly classroom, and I was determined to take notes. "I want you to trust Me just as these birds trust their ability to soar above the earth. I desire that you courageously abandon your need to know the future, and instead abandon yourself to rely upon Me. Though these birds appear to jump to their doom they are equipped with abilities they received from Me. They take no thought, but in complete security they dive, and as they ride the current to the shore below they descend effortlessly, and land safely upon the sand. Go where I call you, even into what you fear, and spread out your wings of faith, completely secure that My Spirit will lift you and direct you as you rest in Me."

Glancing out on the horizon once more, the ocean near the jagged rock was no longer turbulent and ominous, but spread calmly around the rock like a mantle of peace.

Long Live the Queen

"For the time would fail me to tell of Gideon and Barak and Samson and Jephthah, also of David and Samuel and the prophets: who through faith subdued kingdoms, worked righteousness, obtained promises, stopped the mouths of lions...of whom the world was not worthy."

Hebrews 11:32-38 (NKJV)

Unusually warm for this time of year, the cloudless sky greeted us with penetrating brightness. Pulling ourselves up the final step, we were instantly absorbed into the hundreds of by-standers in the courtyard adjacent to the castle. The large crowd, beginning to move as if some invisible hand pulled them down the street, led a regiment of bagpipes and kilt-clad soldiers as they marched in ordered precision, filing out from the castle gate and following the bulging mass through the street.

Except for the modern clothing on the spectators, there was little evidence that we were experiencing a twentieth century event. Swept into the fascination which lay just out of view, we joined the procession, falling in behind the sea of Tartan plaids. Arriving at the scene as the gathering slowed to a stop, we quickly realized two things: there was a palpable excitement rippling through this gathering and we were completely out of visual range to witness any of it!

Requiring a quick and decisive solution to remedy our situation, I instantly found myself being propelled upward and then pinned to the stone wall behind me. My feet danced to find something to stand on, and came to rest on the lip of bricks extending about three inches from the wall. My husband's shoulders mercifully pressed my legs against the wall, preventing me from losing my balance and tumbling into the crowd.

A voice rising from the congestion below me created enough attention to draw faces quickly in my direction, awaiting my answer, "What can you see? What's happening?" With the thrust of a video camera into my hand, my husband followed with the command to be sure to catch it all on tape. Striving to keep my balance while fumbling with the video camera, I tried to look composed, as if I did this sort of thing every day. Scanning the street for a clue to the mystery, I had the brief sensation that we were characters in a story from an antiquated book, gathering here much like the peasants in Scotland might have done centuries before.

A distant cheer rose from the streets beyond us, then from the far reaches of the avenue came the most spectacular sight of human pageantry I have ever witnessed. Four perfectly matched white horses striding together in faultless cadence, introduced a beautiful carriage. Long and billowy feathers peeked out from the carriage windows, waving a greeting as if to prepare us for the sight we were about to behold. Men dressed in ancient regalia bowed as they reached to open the door.

As the white-gloved hand extended to find support, the robe of a Queen, trimmed in white and flecked with black, spilled out of the carriage. A hush, followed by a spirited cheer erupted from the crowd as Queen Elizabeth II stepped out into the street. With perfect poise and the confidence of one born into this destiny, she waved to the masses, turning to face each section, gracing us with her smile. The emotion which rose in my heart astonished me, for this was not my Queen, nor my country, yet the pages of history stormed into my thoughts and I was overwhelmed. Tears falling onto my cheeks, I imagined the wars fought, the prices paid and the sacrifices made to be in a lineage destined for greatness, destined for a throne.

Lost in the vividness of my daydreams, I quickly recovered as another form emerged from the carriage. She was of smaller stature and possessed greater years, but the same confidence covered her as did the robe which covered her predecessor. The same destiny marked the Queen Mother as it did her embellished daughter.

For most citizens in my country, everyday life rarely seems destined for greatness, let alone the elevated position of one born into royalty; however, upon closer inspection one is sure to find noble hearts fighting wars on this soil—wars fought to maintain greatness of another kind: Battles still rage to end the prejudice one group feels toward another because of skin color or differing beliefs. Men and women are born with a destiny to fight injustice and cruelty, while others are born to join in the continuous battle to end poverty and disease.

Prices are being paid daily in this country: Ordinary people gifted by their Creator pour out their lives to lead governments, teach children, and preach the Gospel for the enrichment of others.

Everyday sacrifices continue on in an unending offering to the God of this universe: The sacrifice of lives given to liberate complete strangers in another country who have lived under the harshness of an evil dictator. Parents putting aside their own plans and desires in order to provide for and teach their children that life is a gift and should not be wasted. Janitors and garbage collectors living unnoticed lives behind the scenes while cleaning up our messes, so we can live in sanitized leisure.

Amidst all the pomp and ceremony displayed those many years ago in the city of Edinburgh, it was easy to see greatness and even to applaud it. In the increasing busyness of our western culture, one must make a determined effort each day to unmask the heroes, to search out greatness in the common, and encourage those destined for great acts. The question we must ask ourselves is, "Will we stand on the periphery of the crowd and watch greatness parade by, or will we believe greatness exists in the midst of us, and is waiting for those with faith to live out the destiny God has planned for them?

To Obey is Better than Sacrifice

"Behold, to obey is better than sacrifice…"

1 Samuel 15:22 (NASB)

Putting the last of the freshly laundered clothes back into the suitcases, I carried them to the door and glanced over my shoulder for a final survey of the temporary lodging facility. Aching with relief and anticipation, the transition from TLF to our new home was finally in sight. With no base housing available at this first assignment, we purchased what we affectionately called our "cookie cutter" house in north Dover. After spending significant energy to acquire and file the necessary paperwork for the new public school system, I successfully registered our youngest daughter, Sasha, in her first year of Middle School, and then tried to process the turbulent emotions of sending her older sister off to Bible College in South America. With ample free time on my hands, I set out to satisfy the desire to nest by attacking the boxes that stared at me from every corner of the house.

Relishing in the morning quiet, I reflected over a cup of freshly brewed tea that each of us had moved here with some uncertainty as to what our new roles would be. Encouraging myself with new resolve, I accepted with determination that I would have to carve my role out of the unfamiliar territory known as the military spouse. I had convinced myself in those last weeks back home that this would be an adventure, a chance to embark on a new journey filled with fresh sights and sounds. Married to a minister, I had sufficient experience diving into uncomfortable situations, and this would be no different. I would grow into this new role just as I had during the previous twelve years as a pastor's wife.

As the boxes disappeared and my nesting projects came to an end, I found myself strangely unsettled. Surrounding myself with everything familiar didn't ease the loneliness that began to creep into my heart with ever increasing intensity. Reaching for the last box in the dining room, I pulled out a large object and began peeling off the wad of packing paper. Unable to control the wave of isolation that swept over me at the sight of this particular dish, I sank to my knees and let my heart crumble into pieces.

After several minutes of anguished cries and blurred glances at the ceramic platter, I wiped my eyes and traced each hand written name on the surface. Every woman in our little church had lovingly signed her name to this dish, given on the eve of my departure into the unknown. It symbolized the twelve year journey we shared which encompassed births, weddings and funerals, house warming's and graduations, emotional pain and spiritual growth. These women had known me, and had come to the conclusion I was worth the privilege of walking in friendship with them. This precious group wasn't the only thing I left behind. I had moved across the country from our only son, our step-daughter and only granddaughter, our parents, my job, my home of ten years—everything that identified me as me. Now I was alone, grieving that loss while trying to find my footing three thousand miles away from anything familiar. As if I had unintentionally opened a door to a forbidden room, a new emotion crept into the dark chambers of my heart: Resentment.

In the weeks following my gradual descent into the abyss of resentment, I managed to keep up my daily habit of prayer and Bible reading; however, on a particularly warm morning while mechanically sipping my cup of tea, I perused the Scriptures in search of some words of comfort. As I began reading a section from Luke's Gospel, I was caught off guard by the force of the following passage: "Assuredly, I say to you, there is no one who has left house or parents or brothers or wife or children, for the sake of the kingdom of God, who shall not receive many times more in this present time, and in the age to come, everlasting life."(Luke 18:29-30 NKJV) Though I believed my reservoir of tears had been drained, fresh streams poured freely in gratitude that God could point me to this particular verse.

A new hope emerged that day, but as is typical, God wasn't finished bringing home the first of many deeper lessons hidden in His purposes. As my wounded soul regained strength and faith in His never-failing love, I began to step out into the fringes of the neighborhood and the community on the air base. At what point I began to feel I had accomplished a feat worthy of receiving a nod from the head of Almighty God in return for all I had sacrificed, I cannot say. I will, however, always remember the day God's Spirit set me straight on an important principle of living in the will of God.

Bent over my dining room table all morning, I prayed about my frustration with not yet having discovered what I was to do in this new role as chaplain's wife. After all, hadn't I sacrificed everything to come here? I was certain God had something significant for me to do since I had given up much to support my husband in his new work of ministering to the military community. Impatient with God and myself, I turned the pages until my Bible rested at the story of the life of Saul, Israel's first king.

Whether welcome or not, there are specific moments in time when we come face to face with the uncomfortable truth about ourselves, and that moment headed toward me with divine accuracy: "Has the Lord as much delight in burnt offerings and sacrifices as in obeying the voice of the Lord? Behold, to obey is better than sacrifice…"(1 Samuel 15:22 NASB) As a wave of conviction rose inside me, I felt the painful purpose of God's word expertly cut open my prideful infection like a razor-edged scalpel. "It is easy for others to mistake your sacrifice for spiritual maturity, and place their admiration on you. If, however, you give up what is infinitely important to you in obedience to Me, I will be the One receiving the glory, and your obedience will bring honor to My name." Finding my way to my knees once more, I sensed the sweet liberation which only comes through Divine love softening the hardness of the human heart.

A Wing and a Prayer

"Peace I leave with you, My peace I give to you; not as the world gives do I give to you."

John 14:27 (NKJV)

Life's transitions can at times be stimulating, even exhilarating. More often than not, transitions tend to stretch us, sometimes to the point of snapping. Whether in the camp with the adventurous, or tucked away safely with the things-are-fine-the-way-they-are crowd depends upon your personality, and I suppose your life experience.

Moving to Louisiana in the middle of June constitutes a rather large and uncommon transition, especially if you have lived most of your adult life in the breezy, rainy and otherwise clear-aired Pacific Northwest. As the first wave of humidity produces that curly frizz on top of your head, and the tickle between your shoulder blades is actually a stream of sweat rolling down your back, it becomes clear why local residents affectionately refer to the state as Lou-easy-ana: there is nothing else to do but take it easy in the stifling heat and humidity.

Nearly a year after our move my husband could barely convince me that living in this climate would produce new and appealing qualities in my character. Becoming all too familiar with such things as cockroaches, various lizards (inside the house), poison ivy rashes, fire ant stings and Argentinean ants that join forces to live in super colonies that never die, I feared that I would never again enjoy my longtime hobby of gardening. The quiet routine of my morning devotional time brought the much needed intermission to my ongoing struggle to find contentment. Nurturing myself with my ritual cup of tea, I opened my Bible, and facing a large window overlooking the lush greens of our front yard, tried to make sense of my circumstances.

After trudging through a succession of mornings where I could not manage to utter a word of thanksgiving to God for His goodness and mercy, I found myself muttering repetitious, steely complaints which filed out of my heart like mechanical toy soldiers. Knowing the need to at least try to express my love and thanks to God, I prayed; however, like the toy soldiers, I felt cold and lifeless.

They say confession is good for the soul, providing a clean sweep of the heart through the amazing power of grace and forgiveness. As God worked on oiling the steely door of my heart through His Word, tears of confession streamed down, clearing my vision and invading the pages of my Bible. Several minutes passed in passionate, shoulder heaving waves, bringing me once again to the place where I knew I could offer a prayer in an attitude worthy of the One to Whom I spoke.

Still unable to speak audibly, the Spirit of God gently placed my plea before God, "Peace, Father. I need Your peace." Fatigue began to set in, as it often does following an emotional storm. Blankly staring out the window, I caught a slight movement near the end of our driveway. Landing silently, a large mourning dove paced back and forth across the pavement. As though receiving a tender reminder, I recalled that in Scripture doves represent two incredible things: Peace and hope between God and His creation following the flood, and the Holy Spirit descending in the form of a dove upon Jesus as John baptized Him.

Startled by the immediacy of this metaphorical answer to my prayer, tears flowed freely, this time in thanksgiving to God for hearing me. As I watched the solitary dove wander about on the driveway, peace began to return to my heart. Then, in soundless succession, the most amazing display of the love of God toward this child began to unfold right there in my southern exposure!

One by one, doves began to flutter down from somewhere beyond my view and land next to the single bird. As each one alighted, the depth of peace in my heart increased. Watching in absolute awe as this heavenly object lesson from the Master continued, I counted thirty five doves crowding the end of our driveway, each calmly standing as God's emissary of peace to me.

There have been other difficult seasons since that day, but God's peace has taken up permanent residence here. From time to time, when the storms of life seem to blow incredibly hard, I have noticed something quite extraordinary: A large flock of doves appear on the driveway or atop the telephone wires adjacent to our backyard, reminders of God's peace which transcends earthly difficulties.

Welcome Home

"In My Father's house are many rooms; if it were not so, I would have told you. I am going there to prepare a place for you."

John 14:2 (NIV)

Clouds gathered in the late afternoon humidity, blanketing Tel-Aviv in a hazy glow and generating turbulence in the main cabin of our airplane. Gripping my armrest a little tighter, I focused on breathing slowly in order to calm my racing heart. The pilot's skill in landing the plane with precision as though we had sailed over a glassy sea, initiated a spontaneous round of applause, and more than a few nervous chuckles. Waiting years for the opportunity to visit Israel, the realization that in just a few moments my husband and I would actually be standing on Israeli soil produced an entire flock of butterflies dancing about in my chest. Choosing this particular tour company because of its commitment to help Jews and Christians initiate understanding and find a bridge between us, we would meet together to explore how our religious backgrounds intertwined. Slowly taxiing to the gate, we discussed the interesting twist that the person who awaited us on the ground, who was to be our taxi driver and our host at the end of the tour, was neither Jew nor Christian, but rather Palestinian Muslim. Embracing this opportunity provided through a mutual friend, we were unaware of the multi-cultural awakening awaiting our arrival.

The endless line through customs appeared more like a crowd waiting for a popular ride at an amusement park, crawling along at a frustrating shuffle. With each step forward a sobering sense inched its way into my consciousness. Soldiers of the Israeli Defense Forces, rifles slung over their shoulders, stood watching from multiple vantage points as the line moved along. With so much suffering over the decades in this country, both citizen and foreigner clearly understood the possibility of being in the wrong place at the wrong time.

Standing in the terminal with expectations rising by the moment, my thoughts shifted from solemn to anxious. How can we who live peacefully in the United States understand what it means to live daily with an open and visible reminder that there are enemies who seek to take away our freedoms, and possibly our lives? While the U.S.A. has the reputation of being the great melting pot of humanity, embracing people of every ethnicity and tongue, our history shows that true peace between different races and cultures is fragile and needs our constant sensitivity, if not nationally, then at least individually. Was I to find an invisible barrier between myself and the people of this land as I have found in some parts of my own country?

As I studied the vigilant faces of the soldiers, I was ushered back to reality with the words, "Passport, please." Leaving the congestion of the customs line, I grabbed my husband's hand, ready to embark on this journey. The expanse of the next room was dwarfed by the crowd of dark-haired, sign-bearing strangers, so we probed the area, looking for our names on one of the handwritten signs. The crowd, thinning out as parties found their hosts, left us standing alone in the cavernous room. Propelling him forward, my husband's adventurous spirit spilled forth, and he gave my hand a squeeze, pulling me onward. Rounding the final corner, a middle aged man stepped forward clutching a cardboard scrap which read: "Pastor and Mrs. Knudeson."

As our weary eyes met the dark, smiling eyes of our host, we breathed a sigh of relief and smiled in return. In the next moment, we found ourselves wrapped in the embrace of this gentle man, who, as we found out later, had waited five hours in line to get a taxi permit so he could legally drive us to our hotel. "Welcome Home!" he gently greeted us, and the knowledge that a place had already been prepared for us in this far-away land vanquished any concern of invisible barriers.

Just for the Joy of It

"Come let us worship and bow down; let us kneel before the Lord our Maker. For He is our God, and we are the people of His pasture, and the sheep of His hand."

Psalm 95:6-7 (NASB)

Out of breath in the suffocating humidity of the morning, I flopped down on our patio swing to recuperate from a three-mile walk. Sweat trickling from every pore, I wished for even a slight breath of wind to refresh me. Cicada's, humming their one-note songs, resounded from the trees along the bayou. Resting my head against the swing, I rocked back and forth in an effort to create a breeze. Nearly hypnotized under the monotone spell of the insects, I opened my eyes, adjusting to the bright sun. Straining to focus, I fixed on what appeared to be a flock of purple martins circling overhead. Knowing their nervous habits when their nesting sites are disturbed, I passed it off and examined the feathery wisps of white across the otherwise blue sky. As my thoughts began to wander, another life-lesson made its debut above me, in my very own theatre-in-the-sky.

Thinking nothing of the martin's circular flight pattern, I acknowledged they merely displayed typical bird behavior; however, with little else claiming my vision, I began to notice one bird in particular, whose flight pattern differed from the rest of her flock. The majority, circling once or twice, darted off in what appeared to be an early morning snack attack, returning to the group moments later. Realizing that they were moved by instinct, I wondered at the tenacity required to methodically gather enough insects to feed and instruct their offspring. But my one feathered sojourner was not keeping step with the ballet that danced across my sky-stage.

Higher and higher she circled, wings barely flapping. Apparently riding on a wind current which pushed her onward, she soared upward until I could barely make out her form. Descending, only to rise again with effortless grace, she seemed oblivious to the frantic responsibilities which consumed her companions. With a bit of leisure time on my hands, I relished in the production until insight slowly lifted the curtain from my understanding: Her flight was not out of duty or instinct. Hers was a quest with a much grander occupation; she was flying for the sheer joy of it!

Pushing aside the constraints of hunger and the duty to her nesting brood, she deviated from the routine movements and participated in what inspired her to reach a place where she'd never before flown. Unshackled, she was free to revel in the gift that her Creator had bestowed upon her. Feeling unashamed by the joy I felt in witnessing this silent yet powerful drama, laughter spilled forth from my heart in waves of pure wonder. Although she must at some point return to the earth and its limitations, this was her moment, and she took incredible joy in using her gift to its fullest intent— bringing her Maker joy in an uninhibited act of worship.

An Alteration of Perspective

"For we walk by faith, not by sight."

2 Corinthians 5:7 (NASB)

Rain, falling incessantly since early morning, gathered into large puddles, ripples dancing to the edges with each drop. Too wet and soggy to be outside for more than a moment, I busied myself with a book as hour drifted into hour. With my husband deployed in Afghanistan and our youngest daughter away, I found myself sitting out another Louisiana storm in the company of our dog Amigo. Pausing for a sip of tea, I turned another page in my novel before looking up, my ears aroused at the sudden lull outside. Propelling me instantly into a state of alarm, I encountered a sight never to be forgotten. Moments after glancing up, mind my comprehended that the storm had lightened but my heart pounded uncontrollably as the most dramatic seconds of my life burst onto the scene.

From the vantage point of my dining room window I witnessed an instantaneous shift in our front yard landscape. Trees, normally upright, suddenly bent at near ninety degree angles. Flexible branches, straining as they were thrust into horizontal lines, appeared to flee in panic as the stout limbs of our Chinese Tallow groaned in eerie petition. Winds, forcing through the smallest openings of our house, loudly protested the obstruction to their path. Trying in desperation to subdue the fear that crawled up my spine, much of those final seconds remain a blur except for my instinct to grab the dog and find shelter, sending me headlong into the interior of the house.

Although modern weather equipment can determine with great precision when a tornado is imminent, winds blow where they will, and one's only hope is to find a place of refuge until the storm passes. Crouching in our hallway, terror rose in my throat and threatened to strangle what little reserve I had. As the sickening sounds of objects pelting the house, trees brutally snapping under the strain of the powerful wind, and the very real freight-train roar assailing my ears, Amigo trembled uncontrollably at my side. Feeling the house expand and contract, I knew deep in my heart that I was facing the very real possibility of death, and there was no way to escape it.

Willing myself to breathe slowly in an attempt to control the terror and my thoughts, I prayed through chattering teeth. "Lord, You are my refuge, in You I trust. Help me through this. Please be with me and be with my neighbors. You alone are my refuge." Searching for some comfort, I realized that in my race for shelter I had grabbed my Bible. Letting it fall where it wanted, I looked down at the page and was dismayed to see it had opened to the book of Job, the story of a man who endured not only the loss of all his material possessions, but all of his children and his health as well. I cringed at the thought, yet something deep inside me knew there would be something in the pages to hold onto.

"From the chamber of the south comes the whirlwind, and cold from the scattering winds of the north. By the breath of God ice is given, and the broad waters are frozen. Also with moisture He saturates the thick clouds; He scatters His bright clouds. And they swirl about, being turned by His guidance, that they may do whatever He commands them on the face of the whole earth. He causes it to come, whether for correction, or [to water] His land, or for mercy." (Job 37:9-13 NKJV)

As the force of God's word blew through my heart with greater strength than the storm raging outside, I buried my face in my hands and wept. Following was a time of heartfelt conversation with this Almighty God who had carefully selected His words to gain my attention. Confronted with the frightening prospect that I may not live through the current situation, I found no excuses to deny what I had always believed to be true, but never fully faced: God was in control and I was not. "Lord, are these winds to bring correction or to show Your mercy?" I began. "Please let them be for mercy, but correct me if I need it. You are my refuge and my shelter in this storm."

When clarity comes, it makes no room for self-defense. As though God had whispered into my ear, I felt the sting of truth reveal the true condition of my faith, time standing still momentarily within the chaos of the hallway: "Am I really your refuge? Here in the midst of this storm, with nowhere to go and none to save, you proclaim My words, but am I really your safe haven? What other things have you been trusting in besides Me? If I choose to blow this wind to the point of total destruction, will I be your shelter then? If I call you home this very night, will you trust Me? Will I be your refuge then?"

There was no denying the Source or the impact of this storm-sent message. I was facing two raging tempests simultaneously, both threatening to shred the very fabric of my faith. Unable to move physically, I was held captive to face my fears and the reality of a Creator who demands that our faith be the genuine article. The only authentic response at this point was to admit the foolishness of my self-made, artificial fortress of security. "It's true Lord. I've trusted in my husband to take care of me, the assurance of a monthly paycheck and money in the bank. I've trusted in my health. I've given You lip service and now You are calling my bluff. You have boxed me in and made me face myself—and I am ashamed."

With the last breath of the tornado passing overhead and the returning calm, I was acutely aware of the precise, personal, and practical ways of God. Choosing the exact moment in time to challenge my thinking, He brought me to my knees in repentance. There was no malice in His divine lesson for me, rather the sincere and earnest longing of a Father who desires His child to live the life of faith she was destined to live. Laying my head on my pillow later that night I smiled, realizing that His correction was in fact, also His mercy.

The Road to Jerusalem

"This is My commandment, that you love one another as I have loved you."

John 15:12 (NKJV)

Commemorating the last evening of our tour in Israel with a special ceremony, our excitement soared above the shared longing for additional time that our fellow travelers were experiencing. With prior arrangements in place, the following morning would find us heading to a nearby town rather than boarding a plane to return home. Waleed, the gentle, sign-bearing man who met us at the airport in Tel-Aviv ten days earlier, was more than our driver; within hours we would join him and his family at their home in the small town of Bethany. Leaving our schedule free from formal plans, our hope was to gain new insight from this Arab-Palestinian family who lived in a controversial land deeply divided over religious and ethnic history.

As promised, Waleed arrived at our hotel on time, repeating his embrace and smiling warmly as he loaded our suitcases into the trunk of his dust-laden taxi. Situated three miles from the Temple Mount in Jerusalem, Bethany is an Arab settlement, yet home to ancient sites important to Jews, Palestinians and Christians. Talking with our host on the short drive, we learned that his family was able to trace their ancestors back to the little town for over three hundred years. With fresh insight, this fact began to crack open the door to understanding the complexities surrounding who the land of Israel belongs to. Silently, I wondered how this might affect my own sympathies and perspectives toward this incredible land and its people.

Driving through the maintained streets of Jerusalem and crossing over the boundaries of Bethany, the change in socio-economic level became apparent. Clean streets and groomed flower beds yielded to littered roads and sparse vegetation. Turning into the entrance of Waleed's family compound, the streets narrowed and cinder-block walls took the place of sidewalks. As I clutched my husband's hand a little tighter, I held my breath in anticipation of what lie hidden at the end of the road. Within moments of turning into the narrow gauntlet, the walls gave way to a large, circular courtyard housing three full-size, yet non-descript cement houses. As dust swirled around the taxi before re-settling on the parched earth, a flurry of children ran from the house nearest to us, obviously delighted to see their father return with the cargo of curious Americans.

Temporarily blinded by the intensity of the sun, I guarded my eyes to get a better look at my surroundings. Waleed, sensing my curiosity, explained that the first house in the enclosure belonged to his brother. Next was his house, sporting an apartment directly above which housed his mother. The final home in the courtyard was the residence of Waleed's father, his second wife and their children. Anticipating my next question, he also explained that the woman standing in the doorway of the last house was his step-mother, who was very irritated that Waleed's family received all the American visitors. Smiling in her direction in an effort to extend kindness, she would have none of it, and with a stern look swiftly shut the door. In the web of relationships within the courtyard, Waleed had a younger sister who was the same age as one of his sons.

Carefully placing our luggage inside the first room beyond the entry, our mild-mannered host turned and whispered, "You must keep this door locked whenever you are away from the room—my children are accustomed to receiving gifts from American visitors and sometimes they forget their hospitality." Following Waleed's instructions, we closed and locked the door as we ventured into the living area where the rest of the family sat waiting to meet us. A rug, large and faded, covered almost the entire floor of the main room. While the thick, block walls kept the home cool in the summer heat, the emptiness of the room divulged their poverty. Peeking through the doorways of two adjoining rooms, large beds took up nearly every inch of space. A worn path in the rug led to the kitchen where exotic aromas spilling forth from the small enclave tempted the twinges of our hunger into a steady rumble. Proudly introducing his four sons first, Waleed turned to his oldest daughter and recited the girl's names in descending order. The seventh and youngest child, only five weeks old, was resting peacefully in the hollow of the mattress in one of the bedrooms. Anxious to meet Waleed's wife, Asiya, I skimmed the horizon of dark-haired youngsters and wondered how her life differed from mine. Gleaming floors, visible around the edges of the rug, and the scrubbed faces of her children assured me of her diligence in caring for her family. Silently, Asiya entered from the kitchen where she had been preparing a welcoming feast for two American strangers, a shy smile spreading across her pretty, yet tired face.

Knowing that hospitality is of the utmost importance in Middle-Eastern culture, I was unprepared for the gracious and selfless manner of heart which generated a tangible peace and warmth in this home. In the tradition of their ancestors, everything was done according to the rules of hospitality governing their domestic lives. After our first amazing dinner, for example, while trying to recover from my emotional response to the prohibition of Asiya joining the family meal (she was to eat after everyone else had finished), I followed her into the kitchen hoping to help clean up the mess. Aching with frustration for her situation, I wanted to show her respect and gratitude for preparing such a magnificent meal. Placing some dishes on the small counter space, I gently asked if I could do the dishes. Turning to face me, her weary eyes smiled, and with a kind but firm voice she explained one of the first rules of hospitality: "For the first three days in a Muslim home you are a guest. Once you finish the three days you may help share the work." Not wanting to press against culture, I thanked her for her kindness and the meal, then headed for the living room to join the conversation.

Bethany, meaning house of poverty, was beyond the Mount of Olives which overlooked the old city of Jerusalem and the Kidron Valley. Speaking with passion and delight about the surrounding areas, our host painted a canvas of options for us until it was

114

decided that we would make the three-mile journey on foot from Bethany into Jerusalem, re-tracing the steps of Christ during His triumphal entrance into Jerusalem on the back of a colt. Wearing the appropriate clothing out of respect for religion and custom, we set out early the next morning, quietly making our way through the family compound. Adding to the adventure, two of Waleed's sons would join us on our pilgrimage. As we passed the center of the courtyard and entered the narrow passage directing us to the street, a sweet fragrance of flowers cascading over the walls, masked the unpleasant aromas clinging to the small herd of goats descending from the street above. Walking along the dusty path, I imagined the countless sojourners who steps we now traced. With the walled city of Jerusalem spread before us like a glistening carpet, we passed an enormous crypt-filled cemetery. Standing between the flat-topped, stone tombs, several men adorned in the traditional black Hassidic clothing hovered over a scribe, carefully inspecting his work as he inscribed words to a departed loved one. While ascending the incline toward Stephen's Gate, our journey merged the peaceful, open spaces with the labyrinthine streets of Old Jerusalem. Looking back across the valley, my heart swelled with love for this land and its people—uniquely bound by the devotion to preserve it for the future generations.

A photograph taken by my husband, who at one point lingered behind our little caravan, sums up what I believe is a special metaphor of our time spent sharing hearts, culture and hospitality with our new friends. In it, Waleed's sons, each holding one of my hands, also hold their father's hand as we walk along the road, creating an unbroken chain of hope that somewhere in the middle of all our differences we are uniquely human, created in the image of a God who has linked us inseparably by the fetters of His love. In His infinite wisdom He knew that it was not good for man to be alone, not purely for the sake of procreation but because it is through the vehicle of relationship that we find meaning and value. He designed us with this in mind, and then set us free to discover that in finding relationship and love with one another, we might recognize His blueprint for relationship with Himself.

C a n i n e   I n s t r u c t i o n

You will keep him in perfect peace, whose mind is stayed upon You, because he trusts in You."

Isaiah 26:3 (NKJV)

Mulling over a recent experience, I am convinced that life is rather swollen with enough individual lessons, parables if you will, to warrant our careful attention, and with some thoughtful examination instruction will be forthcoming. While I prefer to ponder the ebb and flow, the heights and depths, today's parable made its way into my heart via the fur-ball known as Amigo, our three year old Australian Shepherd.

Observing our youthful canine with admiration, I have come to appreciate how he is driven by the instincts characteristic of his breed. Intensely loyal and willing to defend against any threat real or imagined, he gives me a level of comfort and security on early morning walks. His ability to focus on a particular object, coupled with his frequent-flying acrobatics in pursuit of the object, make him highly prized for his herding abilities—and a great source of entertainment!

In keeping with Amigo's inherent love of routine, there is a particular patch of grass we consistently stop by to investigate on our daily walks. Consenting to our area leash laws, he has not yet experienced the blissful freedom found in running un-tethered from his restraint. It makes no difference from which direction we approach this green space, for I am alerted to it by the Global Positioning System located on the front of his face: aka, his nose.

Focusing my attention on the lush green instead of the damp, moisture-filled air, I noticed Amigo seemed especially determined to capture the title "alpha dog" from me. In spite of my correction, I was constantly distracted by his ceaseless pulling on the lead. Thinking I would satisfy his longing to explore the marvelous aromas that lie within inches of his canine GPS, I gave him extra leash and allowed him to walk just slightly ahead of me on the grass. What God instilled in the canine olfactory is a mystery to me, and evokes even more wonder when trees are present. Striding somewhere between a speed walk and a sprint, Amigo narrowed in on the tree of choice. No amount of coercion on my part brought him under my control, for the tree was now his purpose in life; nothing could interrupt his focus. Trailing along, somewhat ruffled at my lack of mastery over this animal, the fur-ball parable came into view: There are times when Amigo is perfectly content to walk beside me, giving respect to my authority over him. From the corner of my eye I can occasionally catch a glimpse of him glancing up at me, watching for signs of my approval. Though not as frequent as I would like, the contentment found when dog and master walk in undisturbed rhythm can only be described as peaceful and satisfying.

More often than not, I find Amigo's yearning to lead rather than yield to my desires upsets that satisfying peace I look for in our relationship. While following his nose, he moves in erratic patterns, often blocking my path and sometimes running into me blindly. On

118

occasion he has literally made me unable to move, wrapping me up in the tangle of his leash.

Pausing in the shade of an oak tree, I pondered how I respond to God in similar fashion from time to time. God also desires to lead me through green spaces, walking closely with me and enjoying the satisfaction and peace of an undisturbed relationship. He knows that the safest place for me to be is right next to Him, yielded and waiting for His direction. He longs for my glances upward, like a child seeking to catch the twinkle of approval in her father's eye. Suspecting it for a long time now, I'm quite sure that God understands my great need for contentment which is found simply in His presence.

Marvelous as this is, I need to reckon with the fact that much of the time I respond pretty much like our dog. Instead of finding my repose in the shadow of God's presence, I erratically flit from one urgent item on my list to the next, forfeiting the promise of rest which He offers. Frequently I find myself bound up in a tangle of emotion that only renders me unable to enjoy the love and grace God's Spirit has deposited within me. While God offers me peace and blessing when I follow His guidance, I often push that aside to pursue my worldly concerns. Haven't I learned over the years that when I focus on God the barrage of life's cares and distractions grow strangely dim?

Unwrapping my feet from the tangle of Amigo's leash, I sense a smile spreading across the face of God, and I look up to catch the twinkle in His eye.

How the Mighty
Have Fallen

"For consider your calling, brethren, that there were not many wise according to the flesh, not many mighty, not many noble; but God has chosen the foolish things of the world to shame the wise, and God has chosen the weak things of the world to shame the things which are strong."

1 Corinthians 1:26-29 (NASB)

Standing as tenacious witnesses of strength against the ravages of nature and time, the giant pair of oaks spread wide their branches, offering refuge and shelter for a host of animal life. Sending their roots deep into the fertile soil along the banks of a small creek, I took daily comfort in their demonstration of living endurance as I walked beneath their shady embrace each morning. I found myself immediately looking in their direction when entering the park, their lofty outline signaling something greater than myself—a testimony of the wisdom and power of God.

Filling early with angry clouds, the sky sent forth its warning as the winds blew with steady and increasing force, flinging any item left unanchored into the street and causing the neighborhood to feel uneasy and vulnerable. Neighbors mulled around, securing trash cans and potted plants, yet showing no real signs of urgency. Perhaps they took the warnings issued over the radio and television for granted; the urgency never amounting to much more than the extra work required to keep personal belongings in place. Late in the afternoon, the lull in the steady rain produced a deceiving sigh of relief; however, the torrent of water erupting moments later immediately overpowered any complacency. Within a minute of the terrifying deluge and the eerie silence following it, I sat huddled in the hallway, paralyzed with fear.

Looking in the direction of the park the following morning, my heart sank. The skyline had been altered during the night—the sunny blue sky betraying the chaos of rubble lying everywhere. Not able to distinguish how many trees lay silently among the debris, I instantly recognized the absence of my two sentries from the horizon. Heading out to survey the damage, my path to their location was blocked by limbs and wreckage from the storm; however, I could make out their massive trunks lying mutely across the creek bed. Knowing it would be some time before a path could be cleared and I could get a closer look, I resigned myself to grieve their absence from a distance.

Days later, chain saws cried out continuously from several locations in the once serene park, screaming protests in altered octaves as their chains touched wood. Bark, literally peeled away from many of the old trees by the force of the wind, left scars on those still standing. Countless branches boasted jagged ends where days before limbs and leaves danced in the breeze. Approaching the location of the two giant oaks, I could see how the banks of the creek bed had given way as the tree roots on the uphill side now jutted in grotesque shapes against the sky. Their mighty trunks lay unbroken across the banks of the creek, mute and lifeless. Riveting my eyes upon their transfigured shapes, I wondered at the sadness I felt over their loss.

Jarring me from my soundless reflection, a pair of squirrels, possibly former tenants, chased each other along the fallen trunk of one of the trees. As the water in the creek continued its path underneath the new obstacles, small birds poked around in the mud as though nothing had transfigured their environment. Eternal perspective, like bubbles on the bottom of a simmering pot, surfaced in testimony to the truth held in nature: How often did the scene before me play out in similar fashion within the lives of people, now broken and wounded by life's storms? What causes us to break under the fierce winds of pressure or the whirling debris flung in our direction?

The two oaks had been sinking their roots deep into the earth for generations; surely they had weathered countless storms in this part of the South. Yet their foundation couldn't hold them upright in the path of this particular storm. "You are a bit like that" the quiet Voice in my heart whispered. "Your foundational roots spread out to the Source of life-giving water, yet you often rely upon your own strength to hold yourself up through the approaching tempests. How long will it be, if you continue to depend upon yourself instead of Me, before you too become a casualty of the damaging tornados of life?"

The Master of all nature continued instructing my heart, "I have given you My life so that others will find rest and shelter in your love and friendship. If you stubbornly hold to the soil of your own control and ability, you too will be uprooted, and they will look upon the aftermath of the inevitable damage."

The fate of these two ancient trees held one final lesson for me, though this time easier to bear. Their death has left a huge scar upon the banks of the creek. A partial stump peeks through the pit that once held their roots and trunks, a reminder that the landscape has been forever changed.

Yet there is One who bears the scars of a brutal death during history's greatest tempest: Jesus, who based His earthly life upon the foundation of love His Father had for His Creation, and instead of proudly standing upon His own strength in the storm He trusted His life—and His death—into the purposes of His Father, and has forever changed the landscape of our lives.

The Return

"I am with you always, even to the end of the age."

Matthew 28:20 (NASB)

Tension, forming small stones in my tightening shoulder muscles, moved up my neck, threatening to undo any reserve of composure left in me. I glanced at the clock one more time, acutely aware of the minutes rolling mercilessly into hours and hastening the inevitable encounter with our youngest child. No room for procrastinating, my heart pounded in time with my throbbing head as the approaching test of our relationship as mother and daughter raced toward me. Needing relief, I went out to the backyard to throw the ball to our dog, hoping to find some much needed peace. Blindly tossing the ball in the air, it struck the leaves of our sycamore tree and in turn sent a flock of birds into an exodus from their quiet haven. Typically, birds do not roost in this tree because of its frequently falling limbs; however, as they began their hasty departure my heart stilled upon recognizing their grey-brown bodies.

Merging His compassionate answer to my earlier plea for help, God dispatched His emissaries of peace once again! Landing side by side on the telephone wire above our yard, thirty doves sat in formation, every one of them facing my exact position. Offering my grateful thanks for calming my heart and reassuring me of His presence, I raised my eyes to survey the benevolent display. Sensing a difference overhead, I quickly took a re-count of the feathery bodies. In His sovereign knowing, God was preparing the way before me; He understood that this situation was markedly more difficult than the previous visit of His doves during our first weeks in Louisiana. The mounting need for the emotional strength required to escort our beloved child to a behavioral hospital while my husband remained deployed in Afghanistan receded, and a surge of peace lifted me from the pending turmoil. In keeping with His kindness, God increased the number of His emissaries to remind me that there is nothing I face that can permanently take away that peace, for it is divinely given and cannot be removed by the storms of life.

While I remained in the backyard, the forty five doves sat motionless and silent as they dispatched their peace-filled duty to my soul. Returning to the house to prepare for the upcoming confrontation, I glanced out the sliding door leading to the yard. The wire was empty now, for their mission had succeeded, and my now resting heart gleaned an additional lesson: There isn't a circumstance I face that God's hand cannot touch, not a fear in my heart that His peace cannot calm, and not a moment in time where His love does not surround me.

Mind the Gap

"Therefore, there is now no condemnation for those who are in Christ Jesus."

Romans 8:1 (NIV)

The morning air, still wet from the nightly descent of fog, coated our faces with cool droplets. Tranquility prevailed in spite of the approaching rumble of the train against the tracks. Pulling my sweater up to cover my neck, we walked briskly from the parking lot to the platform, hoping to avoid the rush hour into London. As the rising sun began to evaporate the morning mist, a songbird greeted the day with a soft whistle, reminding us we were not yet in the heart of the city. Anticipating a great day exploring the historic capital, we knew next to nothing about the underground train or Tube as the locals call it, and even less about London.

Our friend and host was a little less enthusiastic about the day, preferring the suburbs to the hustle and bustle of the big city. Observing the passing scenery through the window, my mind wandered back in time, reviving childhood memories of the movie MARY POPPINS. In a particularly vivid scene an old woman is sitting on the steps of St. Paul's Cathedral feeding the pigeons. Singing wistfully as she tosses crumbs to the birds, she presented a very attractive setting to the two young children passing her in the street. Wanting to feed the birds for a tuppence, their banker-father flatly refused to allow them to spend their money on such frivolity. Perhaps in childhood alliance with the two children, and their desire to connect with what appeared an untamable animal, the image found its home in my memory. Or was it their compassion for the old woman whose life seemed to exist around a lonely flock of pigeons? Affecting my vulnerable heart deeply, the outcome of that picture was a life-long desire to visit those very steps of St. Paul's one day, and connect with the emotion I felt during that scene.

Nearing the fringes of London, the train slowed a bit, stopping more frequently to absorb the increasing number of passengers. As the cabins filled with London's workforce, some commuters offered up a smile while passing, but most simply looked beyond me to locate a place to sit for the duration. Inching toward the city's hub, travelers continued boarding until I was squeezed into the last section of space adjacent to the DO NOT CROSS line painted on the floor. Descending beneath the surface of the city, we entered the web of dimly lit train tracks and stations which comprised the two hundred fifty miles of The London Underground.

Studying the sea of humanity that joined our journey toward the center of town, I found faces filled with disconnect, fatigue, anxiety and impatience. While contentment rested upon a small percentage of the crowd, I wondered if the majority wore their expressions as a result of another day spent grinding away in dreary employment. Certainly without a workforce, the city and the train we rode would come to a screeching halt. Sensing there was some deeper reason, I brushed aside the thought, allowing excitement to captivate me once more.

As the stops became more frequent, discharging the precious cargo into the various neighborhoods, a heavily accented albeit cheerful voice repeatedly issued a statement over the speakers. Concentrating, I attempted to single out the words over the hum of voices and engine. "Mind the Trap. Mind the Cap. No, Mind the GAP." With each stop the cheery voice consistently chimed out the same phrase until I could stand it no longer. Turning to my friend, I asked her what the phrase meant. "It means you need to be careful of the gap between the train and the platform as you disembark," she replied. Feeling a bit embarrassed about my lack of savvy, I waited for the train doors to open so I could verify the warning issued by the now irritating reminder. Sure enough, there was a sizeable gap between train and platform at each stop. In the frenzy to board or de-board one could easily catch a shoe in the gap, and be thrown into a dangerous and vulnerable position across the threshold. Nearing our destination, I took care to mind the gap as I stepped off the train.

With both feet firmly planted on London soil, I glanced back at the gap just before the train closed its doors, my eyes darting to the passengers still aboard in route to their destinations. Faces blurring as the train pulled away, a small thought came into focus as it departed: In the journey through life, humanity travels many roads before encountering the unavoidable gap between themselves and God. When we arrive at our final destination and the door opens before us into eternity, we will have no choice but to step across the gap between this life and what lies beyond. For some, the gap will become the symbol of eternal disconnect, fatigue, anxiety and impatience. Some, with a contentment never realized in this earthly life, will step to the other side into everlasting peace because they relied upon the only thing able to bridge that gap: God's offer of salvation through His Son.

Heaven Sent

"She gave this name to the Lord who spoke to her, 'You are the God who sees me'…"

Genesis 16:13 (NIV)

In the weeks preceding our fourth move with the Air Force, stress levels remained well above the norm, partly over the expectation of our first overseas assignment in Spain. Clamoring to learn and obey all directives covering everything from pet regulations to shipping household goods, we received the news with a rather large amount of disappointment: the re-issue of orders announcing our destination was New Mexico, not Spain. With Albuquerque being the government's choice of habitation for us for the next couple of years, we roared into high gear, arranging a whirl-wind trip to look at possible housing options. Finding a newly renovated, old-style adobe home in a neighborhood near the air base, we excitedly made our offer and waited for a response. Adding insult to injury, two weeks before closing on our cute adobe, another disappointment knocked the wind out of our sails; our realtor advised us to back out of the deal, sensing all was not as it seemed with the seller. With less than fourteen days before my husband was to report for duty, I exhausted the rental market in search of a home.

Seven days before leaving, I sent our first deposit to secure the last rental I could find in our price range.

Although it is true that most military spouses eventually learn to flex with the constant changes, uncertainties and joys of military life, I continue to struggle with the plethora of emotions tied to realizing once again that I am unknown; emotions which are inevitably magnified during the first few months in a new location. In the confusion of trying to locate a home, I ignored one of the most important items on my military move checklist—prepare mentally and emotionally for the new surroundings. Renting our new home sight unseen, I was more occupied with packing than anticipating the need for flexibility. So, with half-empty boxes staring at me from one end of the house to the other, I stepped outside to find a bit of solace in nature.

Shielding my eyes from the sun, I surveyed the job that lay before me. Moving into a house occupied by renters for the past decade, the evidence pointing toward neglect glared at me from every corner of the garden. Most of the shrubs, withering under the affects of the devastating freeze from the previous winter, revealed blackened or sickly limbs. The pomegranate trees, reduced to mounds of naked sticks, pathetically offered their shriveled fruit still hanging among their leaves. The trees showed promise but the roses, catching all my attention, stimulated my artistic bent on this bright morning. Looking for something on which to pour out my energies and quell my brooding emotions, the roses seemed to offer a bit of hope.

Inspecting the black, frost bitten stalks on the first rose bush, I remembered with grateful appreciation that the tube of sun block I brought from our last assignment was hard at work protecting my neck from the high desert sun. The rose, obviously quite old, had stalks measuring over three inches in diameter. With so many branches crossing each other, I wondered how it would survive a heavy pruning after the winter damage. Following an hour of careful cutting, I stepped back to survey how things were shaping up. Hands scratched and bleeding from too many close encounters with thorns, I sighed at the rather insignificant dent I had made. I had finally met my match, and the frustration of working so hard without seeing huge results threatened to send me further into my already gloomy pit. Willing myself to continue on, I leaned in close to a certain limb to determine the best angle to wield my pruners. In the moment it took to blink my eyes, a small sparrow landed on the very limb I was inspecting—it was literally inches from my face. Without flinching, its tiny feet holding fast to the limb, the petite bird sat quietly, holding my gaze for several moments. Then, as quickly as it had arrived, it took flight, sailing over the roof and out of sight. Smiling at the thought of such an up close and personal view, a glimmer of hope rose to the surface of my heart, uniting with my thoughts. "So don't be afraid; you are worth more than many sparrows" (Matthew 10:31 NIV).

I am no longer a believer in coincidence. A strategically-sent sparrow—not a robin or a goldfinch, but a sparrow—found its way to my yard; not my neighbor's yard, but my yard, and landed on the rose bush—not the pomegranate, but the rose bush I happened to be pruning at that moment. The King of Heaven who commands the winds to blow and the stars to remain in their courses above, sent His sparrow into my yard to remind me that though I felt small and insignificant in the midst of all the uncertainties of life, He saw me—and He just wanted me to know.

Common Bread

"Therefore, having been justified by faith, we have peace with God, through our Lord Jesus Christ."

Romans 5:1 (NKJV)

Leaving the dimly lit neighborhood in Bethany, we chased the sun westward before turning onto the winding road which ascended Mt. Scopus, one of the seven hills within the city of Jerusalem. Riding in a borrowed taxi, although not exactly legal, made the trip possible as our host's cab was not licensed to drive in this section of the city; being Palestinian meant you could not drive your taxi in a Jewish neighborhood without a special permit. Due to our last minute plans for a gathering, there wasn't time to apply for the necessary papers. Marking the apex of our visit to Israel with a celebratory evening meal, our hosts eagerly anticipated stepping into the tension involved in crossing the oftentimes visible barriers of suspicion between Israelis and Palestinians.

In the sobering silence within the taxi, Asiya leaned near to me, her six-week old infant asleep in her arms. Looking into her kind brown eyes, I remembered her earnest plea spoken in confidence only moments before we left the walled courtyard surrounding her home. "Will you take a picture of my baby and me tonight? I want her to know that her first outing was to the home of our new Jewish friends!" While still nodding my approval, we turned the last corner and followed the long driveway leading to the front of the house.

Still adjusting to the visual clash between the modern homes and the observable ancient history of this land, I did not notice the stares directed our way from the neighboring yards. Scarcely waiting for the engine to stop, we stepped out of the car and into another world. Asiya, dressed in her customary hijab, leaned into the car to extract her baby. "Everything okay over there?" a neighbor called to Daniel from across the lawn. "Yes, we are fine," he returned. Shooting a glance at my husband, he raised his eyebrows at me in agreement; he too felt the uneasiness.

Motioning us forward, Hannah ushered us through the house and onto the patio. Candles, glowing from the perfectly set table on the terrace, cast a flickering light upon the large bread-filled bowl nestled between them. Making my way to the railing, I rested against the balcony and looked out over the canyon. I let my eyes settle upon a shepherd grazing his sheep beneath us, trying to capture a sense of the ancient patterns still being rehearsed on this hillside. Following a few brief courtesies we took our seats: Jew, Muslim and Christian, leaning in close and sharing the contents of the bowl—the common bread.

As we spoke of the fate that summoned our three faiths to this table, our conversation turned toward the topic which brought my husband and me to Israel in the first place: The common root of Christianity and Judaism, and how to bridge the great distance that now existed between them. Listening to Hannah, we learned that many Jews consider Adolph Hitler to have been a Christian.

Expressing my surprise with as much tenderness as possible, she went on to remark, "I thought everyone who wasn't a Jew or a Muslim was a Christian." Sensing the pain in her words, I felt moved to make an apology to Daniel and Hannah on behalf of the Christian world—an apology for the unfathomable misery brought to the Jewish race through the evil actions of one man who was thought to be a Christian. With tear-filled eyes Hannah responded, "I have never had anyone tell me they were sorry for the Holocaust."

Speaking with gentleness and heartfelt openness, our discussion shifted to the topic of peace. With tensions easing between Jews and Palestinians in the previous months, the very real hope for peace occupied everyone's mind. Although they were in the minority, our new friends agreed that peace could be achieved through the daily interactions with neighbors and children. Hope, rising from the hearts of the common people, clung to the desire that reconciliation could be achieved. Perhaps they would live as brothers again after all.

The palpable sense of being on the brink of some great truth rested upon us, as if the heavens bowed low to listen to the echoes of heavenly anthems already in constant proclamation above. Simultaneously reaching our hands into the shared bowl of bread, the symbolism (of common bread) began to form in my mind. Reaching into the bowl together not only satisfied our physical hunger but alluded to a deeper meaning: The hunger for peace is a common desire. Sharing our thoughts one by one, Daniel spoke words from the depth of his heart, filling the atmosphere with absolute solemnity. Quoting in Hebrew from the Old Testament book of Joel he said, "Let us beat our swords into plowshares."

Long ago angels proclaimed over a lonely manger not far from Mt. Scopus that "peace on earth" had finally come, yet one does not have to look too far back into history to understand that peace, once attained, is not always lasting. In mankind's quest for true peace, are we destined to merely talk about it amongst ourselves, or can we hope for more than what we see? In pausing for a moment to reflect upon the difference between the angel's herald so long ago and our "mini-peace summit" that night in Israel, one giant fact rises to the surface: God wasn't merely discussing the desire for peace. He was announcing to the world that He Himself had left His heavenly dwelling place to bring not the absence of war, but the possibility of peace with God.

Canine Instruction Part 2

"Ponder the path of your feet, and let all your ways be established."

Proverbs 4:26 (NKJV)

Enduring the staggering, humid summer heat while stationed in Louisiana and southern Texas for the previous five years, the dry, high-desert air seemed fresh even with temperatures well into the nineties. Moving recently to Albuquerque, my early morning routine of walking Amigo was a welcome respite from the long and tedious ritual of unpacking yet another box pulled inside from the garage. Raised with a love for the great outdoors, and finding myself ambivalent toward the cardboard maze awaiting my perusal, I dug through the box labeled 'dog' and grabbed the leash. More than ready to explore the myriad of hiking and walking trails nestled in the neighborhoods and nearby foothills, I laced up my tennis shoes and stepped outside, letting the warm, silky air massage away the tension.

Rising to the east of the city, the towering wall of the Sandia Mountains creates a comforting compass to both resident and traveler, and then dazzles the masses at sunset with breathtaking vistas of pink and orange tinted mountains. The arid mesa just across the Rio Grande River to the west stretches farther than the eye can see, endless skies enveloping onlookers as though receiving a heavenly embrace. Because Albuquerque is situated at the bottom of the mountain with a gentle but constant downward slope toward the Rio Grande, city planners wisely developed the neighborhoods between the arroyos, or washes, to safely channel the huge amounts of water that can fall during the rainy monsoon months of July and August. Walking trails flank many of the arroyos, often allowing the landscape to develop under the artistic design of nature. Chamisa abounds, nestled happily among many varieties of desert wildflowers in an assortment of yellows, oranges, reds and purples. Cactus and other spiny species also lay claim to the sandy soil, pulling double duty while giving shelter to both mammals and reptiles.

Making our way toward the entrance of a nearby arroyo, I felt the all too familiar tug on the leash, warning me that Amigo was on the scent of something enticing in the dog world. Unfamiliar with the new terrain, he honed in on the mystery aroma, but found the unwelcome sting of a yucca instead—lesson learned. Undaunted by the unfriendly flora, we continued down the path, quickly becoming immersed in the grandeur of the mountains spread out before us like a giant postcard.

Lost in the wonder and beauty of my new habitat, I narrowly missed a close encounter with another dog walker. Excusing myself for the near collision, I felt somewhat annoyed that I had to share this moment with another human. Amigo, on the other hand, was ready and anxious to meet and greet all newcomers with joyful enthusiasm. Reining him in, I returned my attention to navigating us along the path, determined to revisit my private conversation with the Creator of the beauty surrounding us. A difficult move for us, my soul was in need of unsullied focus on things with more significance than the material possessions hidden away in our garage. I didn't have to wait long for some fresh insight.

Eyeing Amigo suspiciously, I noticed he was practically hopping alongside me, yet without protest; his peculiar movements the result of walking on three feet instead of four. Immediately pausing, I knelt down to examine his paw which he hesitantly placed in my hand. On the inside of one of his pads, was a nasty looking thorn with long points deeply imbedded in his flesh. As I carefully removed the intruder, it dug its way into my finger and I marveled that Amigo could walk on it at all. Petting his head, he licked my hand as if to say, "Thanks."

Continuing on, I kept a cautious eye on my furry friend just to be safe. Within minutes my meandering hound was hobbling once again in the shrubs just to the side of the path. Still without protest, he looked up at me with nothing less than a grimace on his face, raising his paw for me to remove not one, but two thorns. Pulling him back onto the path, I turned to resume our walk and brush aside my growing irritation with my dog's persistence in deviating from the path set before him.

The soaking rains of a desert thunderstorm could not have had any more affect upon the dusty soil of my heart than the sudden realization of God's truth. As the thought settled and my mind fine-tuned the illustration, I remembered words penned by King Solomon as he desired to preserve the wisdom he received from God: "Ponder the path of your feet, and let all your ways be established" (Proverbs 4:26). Certainly, my canine companion is not in the habit of pondering his path; quite the contrary: Any interesting aroma will instantly divert his focus from his immediate occupation, sending him into a frantic search of unknown origin. He has managed thus far to avoid any serious damage as a result of his wandering; however, he has often returned limping after meeting up with something unpleasant and unseen apart from the path I had chosen for him. With the increasing intensity of the sun and the truth came a gentle correction: "Broad is the way that leads to destruction, but narrow is the way that leads to life" (Matthew 7:13-14 Author's paraphrase).

Why is it that human nature seems bent on discovering for itself every thorn along life's way? We stiffen at the thought that anyone else should know the correct path for our journey. How often I have sat on the sidelines of the race through this life, my feet bloodied by the thorns I've allowed to pierce my flesh because I chose to ignore the warning signs and go my own way. Perhaps it is because we resent the boundaries. After all, we were created with the freedom to choose.

Returning home from our adventure, I plopped myself down in our overstuffed recliner to think a bit more. Amigo, lying across from me, licked incessantly at the place where I removed his thorns. He bore the wounds, yet tomorrow the pain of today will be forgotten and he will allow himself to be led astray once more by his instincts. I wondered silently, "How many wounds do I need to bear before I accept the truth that I am in need of boundaries?"

My thoughts, traveling back through history to a Man who hung from a Cross; bearing wounds across His head, His back, His hands and feet. The realization that my own wandering nailed Him there comes crashing upon my heart. There is no Divine irritation over the thorns that He has pulled from my life. Instead, I find Him reaching down from heaven, gathering each one as I watch in grateful awe. "Father, forgive them." He whispers, and only then do I catch a glimpse of my thorns woven into a crown, resting upon His head.

Abiding Still

"I am the vine, you are the branches."

John 15:5 (NIV)

The unmeasured sky-spaces surrounding the city of Albuquerque often fill with swelling thunderclouds of massive proportions in the late summer afternoons. If, by Providence, they release their life-giving treasure, it is a certainty that the parched, high-desert soil will push forth in abundance every seed that lay dormant under its sandy blanket. Adapting to the tinder dry conditions brought on by years of drought and high temperatures, native plants have the advantage over the plethora of ornamental trees and shrubs brought to the area over the decades, able to survive without large amounts of water during the driest months. Situated at five thousand feet, the desert can also be a disadvantage to the person who forgets to carry a sufficient amount of water during any form of outdoor activity.

Leaving the house earlier than usual on a spectacular, cloudless morning, I anticipated avoiding the more penetrating rays of the desert sun. Striding uphill for over an hour, my leg muscles strained to propel my body onward. Looking for a shady refuge to catch my breath, I scanned the terrain up ahead: No trees, but a wealth of chamisa. Amigo, ever vigilant, looked up at me with ears perked for any sign of distress. Too far from home to return for my forgotten water bottle, and silently hoping I wouldn't regret my error, I licked my lips and pushed forward.

Striped, blue-tailed lizards raced across my path, heading for the safety of the shrubs just beyond my feet. Glancing up at the mountain in an optimistic search for a patch of clouds to shield me, I spied nothing but endless blue occupying the sky. With my hopes for relief fading, my resolve stirred and, lowering my head in determination, I ignored the sensation of a mouthful of cotton and began to sing, hoping for a distraction from my growing thirst.

Finally approaching the summit and congratulating myself that my goal was within reach, I jogged the last few yards to the turnaround point where the breezes blew against my face, cooling my damp skin. In celebration of my small victory I stopped to take in the mesa, stretching out like brown velvet across the miles, reminding myself that the view was definitely worth the pain. Reaching down to give Amigo a reassuring pat on the head, I caught sight of something on the road ahead of him. Moving forward for closer examination, I took delight in the surprise hidden in the barren landscape; refreshing springs of truth spilling forth over my otherwise parched perspective.

Transforming the sparse silhouette of a scraggly chamisa, was the lush, vibrant green of a second plant growing vigorously under the shadow of the tough, desert native. Large, delightfully fragrant, trumpet shaped flowers rustled gently in the breeze, moving in rhythm as though they knew they had an audience. The perfume-scented air enveloped me, evoking visions of a tropical, flower-filled paradise. Bees hummed softly, gathering pollen in exchange for their

146

life-giving steps. The desire to quench my physical thirst was all but satisfied by the wonder of this common, dry shrub providing shelter from the scorching sun so the beauty of the second plant could unfold. Standing in quiet appreciation, the words of the One who created this marvelous spectacle filled my heart:

"Abide in Me, and I in you. As the branch cannot bear fruit of itself unless it abides in the vine, neither can you, unless you abide in Me. I am the vine, you are the branches. He who abides in Me, and I in him, bears much fruit; for without Me, you can do nothing" (John 15:4-5 NKJV).

At times we are at risk of taking credit for the good things emerging from our lives. The affirmation we receive from others for our successes can occasionally be like a spark touching dry grass, igniting our pride and in the end consuming the chance to demonstrate the gratitude that comes with knowing a rare and special gift has been given. However, as I contemplate the state of that lovely, little plant blossoming in radiant beauty from the mist of the desert shrub, I am humbled by the comparison: We exist and bloom not on our own merit or strength, but because we are enveloped by the love and mercy of a gracious and benevolent God.

I Have a Gift for You

"...the gift of God is eternal life in Christ Jesus our Lord."

Romans 6:23 (NKJV)

With suitcases stuffed into every inch of the truck bed, we came to an abrupt stop in the right lane of a busy highway in the town of Montería, Colombia. Quickly moving to the rear of the vehicle, our driver unloaded our bags and equipment onto the sidewalk, then made a hasty departure from the illegal parking spot. Already stiff from the cramped seating on the commuter flight from Medellín, my legs tingled as I stepped away from the truck and into the moist afternoon air. Our host's home, only a short walk from the noise and confusion surrounding our little group of ladies, beckoned us on. Gathering our belongings, we waited for a lull in the traffic, ran across the road, and made our way down the block to our temporary lodging for the afternoon.

Venturing into this country at the request of my friend, I welcomed the opportunity to explore the culture and gain insight into the ancient and somewhat mysterious history of Colombia, South America. The conference awaiting us drew women from every part of the country, and some, I learned later, had traveled from the southernmost region of Colombia via a thirty hour bus ride.

Following a delightful lunch which included fried plantains and yucca (pronounced yoo-kuh), our host informed us that a second driver had arrived and was ready to escort us on the next leg of our journey to Coveñas, situated on the northern coast along the Gulf of Mexico. Somewhere during this portion of our trip I began to observe that the inconvenience we had already experienced in getting to this point was nothing new for the people who called this country their home. Intense poverty, unhidden along the road, seized my attention. Barefoot women alongside tiny homes flooded from the recent rains, cooked their meals over open fires in heavily shaded yards while children played and animals stood ankle-deep in mud. With this being the norm for many of them, I wondered what my attitude would be if it were my existence.

Arriving at the conference center late in the day, I took in the surroundings of colorfully roofed, cabaña style buildings and palm trees casting their dancing shadows upon the pathway leading to the central gathering point. Upon further investigation my perspective was altered: The grounds must have been quite a gem in their heyday, but now the only redeeming factor was the pool. The temperature, soaring above one hundred with humidity to match, instantly coated my uncovered skin with a blanket of moisture, leaving my clothes to cling unmercifully to the rest of my body. The relentless mosquitoes especially liked our North American blood, and my friend and I were quickly dubbed "carne nueva" an affectionate term meaning new meat. Without further options, we experimented with hiding ourselves under the sheets in order to sleep and escape the unyielding attacks of the miniature blood suckers, only to awaken with dozens of red spots resembling the measles scattered over our faces. During the evening sessions held outside under a large, wooden roof, the mosquitoes were so distracting that the ladies resorted to slapping their ankles just for relief, though I never saw one of them get up to seek refuge.

At one point the food was un-identifiable, with something resembling a sea sponge floating on the surface of my bowl of soup. Following each meal, the dishes were washed in a tub, outside, in the dirt, with no visible soap suds. Cramming together two to a bed, we tried desperately to avoid speaking of the furry friends that shared our dwelling spaces. Replacing showers with a dive into the pool, we abstained from standing in the backed-up water at the bottom of the shower stalls which had the distinct odor of something no longer living.

With inconvenience on every side, each of us from North America (missionaries included) had been reduced to tears at one point. Anticipating discomfort to some degree, we were not prepared to deal with it at this level. Constantly awed by the cheerful, smiling faces of the national women, I was daily greeted with a double dose of kissed cheeks. Not even when heavy rains leaked through some of the ceilings and completely soaked some of the mattresses did we hear even one word of complaint from these beautiful ladies. While I struggled to maintain what little composure I had left, these amazing women were living evidence of a joy much deeper than their circumstances.

Returning to my cabaña one afternoon, I greeted a woman whom I later discovered had occupied a seat on one of the buses traveling for over thirty hours. Admiring each other's necklace, I made an effort to produce small talk with my struggling Spanish skills; then, saying our good-byes, we went our separate ways. I had forgotten about this brief encounter until two days later, while we were packing our bags to return to Montería.

While sitting on the edge of the worn out mattress in my room, this same woman quietly appeared at the door. Inviting her to come in, she shyly she moved toward me. Then, in slow, but perfect English, she said, "I have a gift for you." I was stunned, knowing none of the ladies spoke more than a couple of customary English words such as Hello and Good-bye. Understanding my surprise, she reached toward me, handed me a little box and repeated, "I have a gift for you." Trying to say in my weak Spanish that it wasn't necessary, she simply looked at me and smiled. Opening the box, I looked through misty eyes upon the same necklace she had been wearing a few days earlier. Looking up at her, she radiated delight then bent down to dispatch a kiss on my cheek, and a warm hug. "Demasiado caro!" I said (too expensive!), but she reached down, taking the necklace from the box, and put it around my neck. "A gift for you," was all she said.

During the bus ride home, I learned two facts about this loving woman: She had stayed up late into the night practicing the phrase "I have a gift for you" with one of the missionaries until she had it right. I also learned that the night before she left for the conference she had found her husband with another woman. Yet in all her pain and inconvenience she wasn't thinking of herself, she was looking for ways to share what little she had to bless and serve someone like me who had dozens of necklaces at home. Out of her poverty she had made me rich, and touched my heart forever.

I have a gift for you—isn't this what our God says to each of us? In all the pain and inconvenience of the Cross He wasn't thinking about Himself, He was looking for the only way to share eternal life with us. Out of His poverty, He has made us rich—and has changed our destiny forever.

A Bird in Hand

"Are not two sparrows sold for a penny? Yet not one of them will fall to the ground apart from the will of your Father."

Matthew 10:29 (NIV)

Years ago, while living in the Pacific Northwest, my husband and I endeavored to rescue a young Green Heron that appeared to be abandoned near the bushes in our front yard. After several unsuccessful attempts I picked up the phone to implement Plan B: Call the Audubon Society. Placing an immediate halt to our intervention, the voice on the other end of the receiver issued this warning: "Never attempt to rescue a baby bird that appears to be in distress or abandoned—especially a bird such as a Heron. That little bird could put his beak through your skull if he wanted to!"

Strolling up our street in Albuquerque a decade and a half later, this somber warning echoed in my ears as I happened across a tiny, nearly invisible hummingbird stranded on the sidewalk. His flight feathers were intact, but it was plain to see he was in distress and unable to fly. I stood hovering over him for several minutes, anxiously in need of a solution. Nearly 8:00am, the intense morning sun would soon rise over the neighboring homes, sending the blistering heat directly upon this miniscule member of the bird family. In the midst of his frantic chirps I steadied myself, and walked on.

Finding no joy in my daily exercise, the reality of what I would most likely find when I returned home produced more than enough remorse to dampen my enthusiasm. Vowing that if I found him alive, I would resolutely ignore the Audubon warning and try to rescue the tiny victim. An hour later I turned the corner, hurrying back to the location of the baby hummer. As I expected, the sun's rays beat down on the sidewalk, converting it into a cement griddle. Making an earnest search of the area where I had left him to fend for himself, my thoughts rehearsed the possible scenarios, but there was no trace; he was gone. With a sinking heart I turned to leave, feeling a mixture of hesitant relief and growing regret that I had not attempted to rescue him earlier.

Cutting across the rock-strewn parking strip, a tiny sound reached my ears from the curb below. Rejoicing in the destiny of the moment, the petite fledgling rested a few feet from his original location, nestled among the smooth landscape rocks! Already noticeably weaker, his little body shook with every frenzied chirp. Bending down to scoop him up in my hands, I thanked God for sparing this little one and placed him in a broad yet protected niche of the tree he had obviously fallen from. Wondering if I had done the right thing by touching him, I promised myself I would return later in the day to check on his condition; however, when the appointed time came he was nowhere to be found. I've often wondered if my efforts to intervene in the life of the hummingbird proved merciful or fatal. It is something I will never know.

Working in our garden several days later, I went to retrieve a ball from an obscure section behind a two foot retaining wall packed with gravel and tall grass. Reaching over the wall, I spied a line of tiny bodies racing along the back fence, ducking under the cover of the grass. Believing I had just spotted mice, I looked again, only to discover the mice were actually a covey of eight baby quail. Quickly taking action, I surveyed the unkempt section of ground to see if it was a safe nursery to raise the chicks. Without protection from predators, which in this part of the country include rattlesnakes, hawks and other predatory birds, the risks outweighed the benefits. After constructing a temporary lean-to shelter and placing a shallow pan of water nearby, I stepped back to let the chicks investigate the new additions to their refuge. The parents sat quietly atop the fence surrounding the little triangle-of-ground-turned-nursery, eyeing me suspiciously.

Scattering small seeds and filling the water pan daily for nearly two weeks, I was eager to help them survive. Venturing out quite early one morning to inspect their progress, I could find no visible life within the walled nursery. Knowing the babies were still too young to fly, I feared the worst and sat down on the wall. In a flurry of ruffled feathers, baby quail shot forth, running in their characteristic single-file line-up, wide-eyed and erect. Audubon warnings echoing inside my head, I examined the shallow pit the parents had hollowed out next to the fence. Lying closely together, they sheltered their brood securely under their wings each night. Obviously too close for comfort, I had upset their peaceful morning by intruding into their personal space.

Backing slowly away from the enclosure, I noticed that the covey looked a little thin. After taking a head count, I realized there were six, not eight, chicks in the playpen. A quick re-count proved my math skills were still functioning correctly, and leaning back against our cherry tree, the realization of the course of nature sent goose-bumps up my back. This pair of quail decided to hatch their chicks within an enclosed area sadly lacking any sort of escape route before the chicks could either jump or fly over the short walls. In a matter of days, weeks if they were lucky, each chick would fall victim to their position on the food chain. Attempting to aid them on their journey to adulthood was simply a placebo for the harsh reality that awaited each of my feathered friends.

With the passing days, the chicks disappeared one by one, and I became somewhat melancholy about the whole situation. I blamed the foolishness of the parents for choosing such a dangerous place to raise their young. I blamed the predators for their cruelty; certainly there were other creatures more suited to becoming a meal—ones that had no fur or feathers and had nothing cute or endearing about them. I blamed myself for lacking the ability to provide anything that would effectively hide them from their enemies. This was one biology lesson I preferred to learn from a textbook rather than through life experience. Imagining the facial expression of a certain

Audubon employee produced much regret; somehow it felt like a day of reckoning.

Heading outside to water the garden one afternoon, I mindlessly let the water pool at the base of a rose bush. As the watery spray bounced off an adjacent bush, four bodies, two large and two small, darted out from under the plant. Startled by their sudden movement, I moved back to trace their flurry and determine what un-announced visitors I had inconvenienced. To my surprise and delight, the adult pair of quail and the two remaining chicks sat huddled together, sheepishly peeking through the leaves. Surviving the dangers of their rocky prison, they had since gone A-W-O-L! Knowing there was a small window of time before they would leave the relative safety of our backyard to venture on into the larger world of our neighborhood, I felt a certain satisfaction in knowing they had endured, as if I had something to do with this miraculous ordeal of survival.

Making the final preparations for dinner that afternoon, I listened to the cacophony of bird songs through the open window. One chirp, however, rose above the others until it reached a rather panicked pitch. Suppressing the impulse to engage in any further bird affairs, I re-focused my energies on the salad dressing, hoping nature would rectify the situation without my assistance.

"It's okay sweetie, don't worry. Everything will be alright," I heard my neighbor speak gently, unaware of the object of her soothing words. "Everything okay?" I offered softly, peeking through the window. Shaking her head, she motioned for me to come outside and assist her in what appeared to be a clandestine attempt at some sort of rescue. Bracing myself, I abandoned my kitchen duties and went outside to meet her at the fence. Peeking down on her side of the four-foot wall, I saw the two adult quail and one chick huddled together in the corner of the side yard, chirping nervously. The loudest chirps, unfortunately, came from the other side of the fence in the front yard. Moving quietly in the direction of the panic, I found the smaller of the two chicks trapped between the wall and the huge tree nestled up against it. "What do we do?" my neighbor asked, clearly in distress over the whole situation. Quickly assessing the circumstances, I whispered, "We have to catch the chick and return it to the parents. It will never survive out here alone." She was unwilling to do the job as she knew that to handle the chick could place it in the untouchable category with the parents. As visions of a lock-down room for those who ignore Audubon directives flashed across my mind, I ignored it and moved into rescue mode. Scooping up the frantic, feathered chick, I concentrated on not squeezing him too tightly in the urgency of the moment, and ran to my neighbor's backyard to deliver the baby to its parents.

Stopping about ten feet away, I knelt down, the baby chick pecking feverishly at my hands in an attempt to free itself from its unknown captor. As I opened my hands to release the chick, he struggled momentarily until he was completely free, and in an instant ran directly to the parents, diving under the refuge of their wings.

Without an attempt by the parents to refuse the chick's desperate lunge for safety, I gradually backed away, leaving them to recover.

A week passed with no further sighting of the quail family, and I found myself relying on the goodness of the Creator instead of human intervention to care for the most vulnerable of His animal kingdom. Early one morning I went outside to cut some roses for our table, trying to keep up with the steady harvest of blooms. After cutting several stems, I paused to search for the best remaining buds. On the fence just beyond the roses and directly opposite my face sat an adult quail, fully adorned in his Mohawk-style headdress. Surprised to find I had company, I whispered to him, "Well, what has become of your children?" As if prompted by my question, a rustling from under a bush produced two miniature versions of the fence-sitting parent, racing from their cover toward the side yard. With a bit of divine choreography the second adult flew up from under the roses and perched beside her mate. They sat silently, staring at me for several seconds as if to offer me a grateful look and a heartfelt thank-you, and then joined their chicks on the side yard. Sensing wholly the blessing of the moment, I smiled in appreciation of our benevolent God who, perhaps, was smiling with me.

Recently, I've taken the opportunity to reflect back on this chance encounter with some of God's creative best. I am struck deeply by the similarity of our desire to rescue a helpless, suffering creature and the divine rescue God has made through the Cross of His Son. When we were at our most vulnerable point, prisoners behind the walls of our sin, God sent His Son to us. We were stranded along life's path, waiting to succumb to the scorching heat of our own fallen nature, with no help in sight. The dangers and the unseen enemies lay hidden, waiting for darkness so they could launch their attack upon our souls. It was from the midst of this darkness that the Son of God, shortly before being ushered into the darkness of His own death, cried these words:

"O Jerusalem, Jerusalem, who kills the prophets and stones those who are sent to her! How often I wanted to gather your children together, the way a hen gathers her chicks under her wings, and you were unwilling!" (Matthew 23:37 NASB).

There is no way to measure the length and depth of love God has for His creation. Yet we fight and struggle and even peck at the very hands of God as they encircle us to lead and protect us from harm. How great is the truth that in spite of our own unwillingness to accept His rescue, He continues His relief efforts on behalf of all His children, waiting for the day when He can release us into the fullness of His love and forgiveness.

Clouded Revelation

"He has delivered us from the power of darkness and transferred us into the kingdom of the Son of His love, in whom we have redemption through His blood, the forgiveness of sins."

Colossians 1:13-14 (NKJV)

Wonder cascading over me, I watched in silence as the east wind slowly blew the clouds down the western slope of the Sandia Mountains like a graceful waterfall. The jagged cliffs, often concealed by the brightness of the desert sun, stood exposed for what they were: lonely and inaccessible. Adding to the compelling atmosphere were the twenty-plus radio and cell phone towers erected strategically on the highest ridge. Lingering for several moments to fully absorb the unfolding drama, a chilly breeze swirled around my feet, tossing leaves into the air in circular patterns. My eyes pouring over the remote cliffs, I noticed the clouds had enveloped the majority of the steel towers, leaving them partially shrouded with only their narrow tips peeking through the misty white. A melancholy loneliness settled over me, the type which invades the human heart after a soul has been misjudged or forsaken.

Brushing away the goose bumps from my arms, I walked a few yards along the arroyo, searching for something deeper than a rehearsal of forlorn memories from past rejections. "What is it that can take an otherwise majestic life and shroud it in misty despair?" I mused. As a ray of sun broke through the celestial awning, the intensity of truth cleared away the clouds from my thoughts: The human soul was created for the purpose of worship and fellowship with God. As sin entered the world through man's disobedience, the cold wind of doubt, despair, and loneliness blew into the human heart. No longer enjoying the intimacy the Creator intended to share with His creation, man was plunged into the foggy reality of a broken world, seemingly left alone to navigate the storms and tempests that eventually blow through each life.

Returning my attention to the mountain, I noticed the clouds parting briefly high up on a particular portion of the rock face. Unable to resist the gratitude rising from my soul I shouted, "Amazing! Thank You God!" Etched deeply into the mountain stood the exposed striations which time, wind, and water formed into the shape of a permanent, enormous cross—a landmark for the entire city of Albuquerque to observe!

While we cannot deny the weathered scars our own sins have etched upon our hearts, we also cannot deny that we are not left alone to navigate the storms of life. God, in His infinite mercy and love, sent His Son to bear and to become the sum of every sin recorded throughout history. As the dark clouds descended upon His holy corpse that day, the Father lovingly blew back every penalty, every consequence that mankind deserved.

Instead of His wrath we can receive His mercy. Instead of gloom and loneliness we can receive His light and fellowship. No longer must we suffer under the weight of our own tendency to do wrong because we have been set free to live this life, enveloped in the brilliance of His lovingkindness and peace. God has set our feet upon the high places of His love, far above the clouds of despair, and He is beckoning us to join Him as He waits to walk us through the waterfall of His forgiveness.

The Anointing

"Praise be to the God and Father of our Lord Jesus Christ, the Father of compassion and the God of all comfort, who comforts us in all our troubles, so that we can comfort those in any trouble with the comfort we ourselves have received from God."

2 Corinthians 1:3-4 (NIV)

Living in Louisiana contributed to my appreciation for what defines a sultry summer evening; however, sitting under the tin roof of this open-air conference room, I realized my definition was lacking. A person cannot truly appreciate the sticky, suffocating, intensity of a mid-summer, coastal twilight in Colombia until one experiences it firsthand.

As the evening sky began to drape shades of lavender and grey, the oncoming darkness wrapped itself around us in similar fashion to the thick, moist air. The handmade banners lining the imaginary walls of our room mirrored the messages which came passionately from the lips of our speaker, Ruth. Occasionally, a soft breeze gave momentary relief from the sweat, tracing patterns like small streams down my back.

From my vantage point looking out across the sea of faces crowded onto the pavement, all eyes were fastened upon the message displayed on the screen directly above Ruth. Expressions of hope spreading across each face revealed an inner thirst for answers to long held questions; a solemn stillness in the midst of the oppressive heat spoke of their patient endurance to what many of us would deem intolerable.

With darkness continuing its relentless pursuit of light, I struggled to stay focused on the timing required to execute a flawless PowerPoint in sync with Ruth's material. Each pause in the message fostered a reverent hush, giving the sense of Heavenly approval descending softly upon us. Thus united in thought and heart, we effortlessly dismissed the barriers of language and culture that had initially appeared as a hindrance.

In every personal journey through life, defining moments arrive, bringing clarity and pointing us to divine truth previously hidden from our understanding. In our obscure little conference room, one of those defining moments, cleverly wrapped in an earthly parable, was heading in our direction.

Continuing my vigil to stay alert, I suddenly experienced the brief sting of something all too familiar to someone with life experience in Louisiana. I reached down to gently brush away the tiny, winged vampire feasting on my unprotected ankles, wary of drawing attention away from Ruth. After several attempts to find relief, I caught a glimpse of a woman across the room from me, her hands mimicking mine as she quietly brushed away another intruder.

Stealing a moment to glance upon the reverent faces again, the hopeful countenances had converted into strained expressions, resolutely determined to give respect to their speaker in spite of the dusky distraction. Then, as if prompted from an unwritten script, hands began slapping ankles and legs all across the audience. As the onslaught reached a fevered pitch, our beloved speaker fell prey and began slapping her ankles along with the crowd. The humor of the moment caught on, and the room erupted in unified laughter. Ruth, being the missionary, never missed a beat and continued delivering her message with her usual passion and candor, however, my inclination was to run for cover.

Silently emerging from the ocean of slapping hands, a woman knelt down in front of Ruth. As the rest of the women continued on in their struggle, I witnessed in that brief moment a heavenly message about the God who seeks to communicate His truth to all who will receive it. The humble saint kneeling before our speaker opened a bottle of mosquito repellant, rubbing it gently on Ruth's feet while ignoring the bugs assaulting her own legs. Without a word, she ministered relief and healing to another who was also selflessly giving for the sake of others. As our speaker received the encouragement to continue on through the anointing comfort of the bug repellant, she flawlessly delivered God's message with both strength and humility.

Long ago, another woman silently knelt before the King of Heaven and anointed His holy feet with costly ointment. It was a gesture that incurred criticism and disgust from those who followed Jesus, but evoked kindness and praise from the lips of the Master. Those who were His closest friends missed the ache in the heart of the Son of Man: His human need to be comforted as His hour of testing approached.

Through the selfless action of one woman, Jesus received anointing comfort to strengthen and sustain Him in the fulfillment of God's precious message of salvation. As He endured plots for His destruction along with rejection and betrayal, perhaps through Mary's actions Jesus realized a tenderly disguised encouragement from heaven to continue on to the Cross.

Reflecting upon the gestures of these two very different women, I am pressed to consider how my own actions have offered, or possibly withheld, some form of comfort to someone who suffered silently. Through witnessing the simple action of pouring much needed ointment upon the feet of one in need, I have learned that the opportunity to minister comfort to the heart of Jesus becomes a reality through the selfless act of serving one another.

Glory Road

"And we, who with unveiled faces all reflect the Lord's glory, are being transformed into His likeness with ever-increasing glory, which comes from the Lord, who is the Spirit."

2 Corinthians 3:18 (NIV)

Trees aflame with color; crisp breezes forcing another layer of clothing and an extra blanket on the bed; the approaching holidays—everything seems more vibrant and alive in the fall. With the changing weather new birds migrate into my yard in their frenzy to consume nature's final yield. The rose bushes, impressive with their late display, push forth their last glorious blooms. As the march toward winter slowly invades, various trees in our neighborhood flaunt their ability to mimic the radiance of the sun; their bright yellow leaves glowing in the early morning light. While spring unashamedly speaks of new life and re-birth, fall shouts of the glories of our Creator unlike any other season.

Making my way through the park on a perfect fall morning, I headed toward my favorite arroyo. Living in the city, I am always on the look-out for places and spaces that provide an atmosphere of solitude and peace. Affording a view of the entire seventeen mile range of the Sandia Mountains, the arroyo is scattered with a certain species of shrub commonly known as chamisa. Ordinary and scruffy looking, there isn't much about chamisa that would attract the attention of anyone, except perhaps small birds seeking shelter or the banquet of autumnal seeds. Without fanfare, during late fall they boast a profusion of small yellow or white flowers, filling the air with a pungent, sweet-sour scent that wreaks havoc on sinuses. In addition, their long, gangly stems begin to fall over with the weight of the blooms, exposing the internal heart of the plant.

Pausing for a moment while Amigo inspected a particular plant, I studied the antics of the tiny chick-a-dees, almost invisible among the stems of the chamisa. Moving on, I noticed that several of the rocks imbedded into the path were gleaming in the morning sun. Stirring something within me, yet before I understood the compelling emotion, I was immersed in a most remarkable scene. Dozens of chamisa lining the path ahead of me were transformed by the sun, backlighting and altering their mundane appearance into glorious, golden torches. The dirt path, entirely transfigured by their beauty, appeared as the kingly entrance to a splendid palace. Unable to look away, a palpable reverence settled upon me, leaving me awe-struck by the stunning surroundings. Without effort my thoughts gave way to a familiar passage from Scripture, "And the street of the city was pure gold, like transparent glass. But I saw no temple in it, for the Lord God Almighty and the Lamb are its temple. And the city had no need of the sun or of the moon to shine in it, for the glory of God illuminated it, and the Lamb is its light" (Revelation 21:21-23 NKJV). My heart, swelling with gratitude that God had chosen this seemingly insignificant little path to unfold such a significant picture of His truth to me, resonated in heavenly anthems of praise.

While walking through the arroyo again days later and reflecting on the emotion and wonder of my earlier encounter, my soul captured a heavenly reality which formerly lay hidden beneath the glory of that moment: In some ways the ordinary, scruffy chamisa reflects the story of each of us. We come into the world ordinary, untidy, and most likely screaming that we've been removed from the comfort and peace of our mother's womb. By the world's standard, few of us emerge into the category of extraordinary. Most of us continue on as average and ordinary, lacking any visible signs of being exceptional. The weight of life tends to bend us downward, exposing our vulnerable hearts to the world, and tempting us to become experts at disguising this fact. Often, simply because of the cares and challenges we face over time, the fragrance of our lives which was meant to be a sweet aroma to our Creator, becomes mixed with the sour scent of sin, compromise and suffering. Looking back down the path of our lives it seems we don't have much to show for our time here. Just the drab, ordinary moments of lives lived in the everyday pursuit of purpose. But there's more than meets the eye here.

At our invitation, this Creator-God, this "Lamb who is the light" changes everything! Because of His love, He transforms our ordinary scruffiness into something worthy of a King. He places His own glory upon us so that we no longer reflect what is ordinary. By His Spirit we become extraordinary and precious as children of God. The cares of this life that have weighed us down and bent our spirits are carefully removed by His power and grace, allowing us if we choose it, to rise upward. The once foul smelling odor of our lives is also changed, and our gratitude to God permeates the world with His sweet fragrance. As the final touch, God shines His light upon the fading flower of our existence, converting our lives with the same radiance of His love so that we reflect His light to others. Yes, without question, everything seems more vibrant and alive in the fall!

Prescription for Awareness

"The Word became flesh and dwelt among us…"

John 1:14 (NASB)

Heading west in our rented Citroen, the sunlight sparkled against the calm Mediterranean Sea. With a perfect autumn morning before us, I soaked in the dreamy warmth coming through the windshield. In celebration of our fifteenth anniversary, we were living out a ten-day adventure in the Andalucía Province of Spain, home of my paternal ancestors and the culmination of a thirty-year dream to set foot on Spanish soil. Driving south from Granada to the Sea, we headed west along the southern Mediterranean shore to our final destination for the day in Marbella. Completely distracted from my navigational duties by the glorious weather, I let my imagination loose, trying to picture the citizens who first named these ancient towns with romantic names such as Salobreña, and San Pedro de Alcántara. Noting the similarities between the arid landscape and my childhood home along the once undeveloped miles of Southern California coastline, I reconnected with sweet memories of beach excursions and treasures discovered in the sand.

With nothing blocking the view of the Sea on this particular stretch of road, I nestled back in my seat, completely relaxed and content.

"Can you see that mountain over there? There, on the other side of the Mediterranean. I wonder what part of the world that is?" my husband mused. Straining my eyes to see what he was referring to, I could make out the impressive outline of a mountain range on the far side of the sea. Without hesitation I grabbed the map, quickly determining our location, then confirming my hunch that we were within driving distance of the Straits of Gibraltar. Searching my mind's dusty filing cabinet labeled "Jr. High School History", I remembered that the Straits were strategic because the continents of Europe and Africa were only separated by this narrow strip of sea—less than twenty miles across. "That's Africa!" I nearly shouted. Always on mission for a new adventure, my husband took the next exit to investigate the possibility of finding a ferry to take us across.

Within an hour we were parked in a large lot in Tarifa, the southernmost town on the Iberian Peninsula and home to some of the world's greatest windsurfing. The ferry company, informing us that yes, it was indeed Africa—Tangier, Morocco to be exact, explained that there were daily ferries to and from the other side of the Straits beginning at 8:00 in the morning. Immediately purchasing our tickets for the following morning's ferry ride, we languished at the thought of waiting eighteen hours for a guided tour, complete with a Moroccan host who would lead us through the maze of tangled streets within the Kasbah. Hopping back in the car to retrace our path back to Marbella for the night, we marveled at our good fortune in finding an additional escapade to share.

Pulling ourselves out of bed without difficulty early the next morning, the excitement took hold as we quickly packed our belongings and set out again on the road to Tarifa. As we lined up to board the first ferry of the day, I took stock of our touring companions: a British couple, two American sisters, a rather sleek looking French woman in a very short dress, and a young couple who, after befriending us, confided that they were from Israel and didn't want to risk sharing that piece of information with the rest of the party in case it created an incident in the predominately Muslim populated Morocco. Concluding that a smaller group was a bonus, I silently celebrated there would be less time waiting in lines and more time for cultural insights. Twenty five minutes later, we took our first steps in Africa.

Docking at the quiet port, the sun was already beating heavily upon us, prodding us to don sunscreen and sunglasses. As the line for customs wrapped around the ferry's deck, we inched our way forward, passing through the check-point without occurrence. Scanning the area for signs of our tour guide, I noticed a rather tall, caftan-wearing man striding toward our group. Having a gentle face, he spoke English rather well in spite of his heavy accent. With the city stretching out before us and many sights to see, he hurried us along to our small bus, whetting our appetites for adventure as he rehearsed our itinerary. We drove around the outskirts of the city, viewing outdoor markets, the former homes of rich and famous Americans and the palace of the Governor. Interesting and informative, yet we were anxious to get down into the maze of streets and touch, taste, and smell everything Tangier could throw at us in eight short hours. We were not to be disappointed!

Following a flurry of Arabic words, the driver jerked the bus to the curb and announced we had arrived at a very famous spot. Pressing together to reach the coveted "best spot to take a picture," we stepped out onto the dusty ground, necks craning to see what all the excitement was about. As the sudden waft of fresh camel wove its magical charms, I coughed and stepped aside, hoping to find some fresher air up-wind from which to take my photographs. The first to ride was one of the American sisters, and while I anxiously awaited my turn, I was amused to discover the ride lasted for one leisurely lap around the small, dusty lot! In spite of one couple in our group declining the privilege of sitting atop the very uncomfortable saddle, swaying back and forth for sixty seconds and smiling sheepishly for the camera, we tackled our first official tourist site in less than fifteen minutes.

Weaving our way around the city, we experienced snake-charmers, Moroccan carpet weavers and impoverished vendors who followed us for blocks, pleading with us to buy something, anything. Sitting cross-legged on over-stuffed pillows, we tasted amazing Moroccan dishes and snuck photographs of Berber women who instantly responded with a flood of Arabic words. Passing brightly painted doors and museums in the Kasbah, we finally stopped at what looked like the back door of a vacant building. Informing us in hushed tones that we had arrived at the apothecary, a slight, dark haired man swung the creaky door open and we filed inside.

Stepping inside the enormous building, we were ushered to narrow, wooden benches forming a circle in the center of the room, and encouraged to take our seats. Insignificant, rectangular windows shed light from each end of the large room as swirls of dust floated across the hazy glare. The white walls, sparsely decorated with an occasional painted palm branch or ornate ceramic plate, bore shelf after shelf of jars and bottles containing unidentified powders, leaves and seeds. Taking in the otherwise sparse surroundings, I barely noticed a second man walking to the center of our little circle, waiting patiently for all eyes to focus on him. Receiving a nudge from my husband, I caught the intended message that the demonstration was about to begin. For well over an hour the gentleman became increasingly animated, explaining in various levels of English proficiency the contents of each and every jar and bottle in the apothecary. It was about the time when legs and other parts of the anatomy turn numb that the concluding demonstration was prepared.

Opening the final jar filled with a white, powdery substance, our host scooped out a small portion and wrapped the contents in a small section of cloth. With a quick twist he successfully contained the power inside the cloth, and walked toward my husband who was seated nearest to him. Foregoing explanation, he placed one hand behind Jason's head and with the other he thrust the freshly wrapped powder under his nose and commanded "Breathe!" Obediently, my husband followed orders and took a large whiff of the cloth ball. One by one the ball was thrust under every nose in the room, and upon hearing the command to "Breathe!" we dutifully took a deep sniff of the unknown prescription. Sitting speechless for several moments, a whisper began to circulate that we were all either absolutely foolish or quite naïve to allow such an exhibition. Fortunately, no one suffered any ill effects, and it was then explained that the careful mixing of this particular powder was for the relief of sinus problems and headaches. Purchasing a bar of miracle soap at the end of the demonstration, I was relieved to finally exit the apothecary, and made a mental note to write a letter of appreciation to the FDA when we returned to the states.

To allow ourselves to be challenged and stretched beyond our boundaries or comfort zone is a healthy exercise—certainly the visit to the apothecary fit the bill. To expose ourselves to another's culture and to see firsthand how poverty, religion, disease and governments affect the lives of those with whom we share this world can only help us to understand, and unite us in the common bonds of humanity. To appreciate and value the scope of what God undertook in putting on human flesh as the means to offer us understanding and unity with Him, we must realize that it was a voluntary obedience on the part of God. He stepped out of the eternal and into the temporal world in the Person of Jesus Christ to be stretched to the point of death; so that we would have the certainty of a true and eternal bond with the One from whom all race, culture, and uniqueness originate. Certainly, this too fits the bill of stepping outside of One's comfort zone.

Canine Instruction Part 3

"Do you not know that in a race all the runners run, but only one gets the prize? Run in such a way as to get the prize."

1 Corinthians 9:24 (NIV)

The crisp, cool air surrounded my face, brushing my skin with a gentle breeze. Clouds hung tightly over the mountain ridge, and I watched in anticipation while the sun's rays scissored through, sending finger-like beams across the foothills. A bird-symphony erupted in praise as the morning unfolded in glorious beauty.

Preferring to walk uphill at the beginning of my walk, I set out for the first of three parks which connect the four mile route near our home. Amigo, always ensuring I employ sufficient effort to keep him from pulling me forward, was tethered to my hand, and eager for his daily romp. Absorbing his contagious enthusiasm, I smiled to myself, knowing that I would not be the consistent walker that I have become if it weren't for my furry companion. With the magnetic lure of the mountains before me, I reveled in the fact that after six months I barely noticed the extra strain of pushing uphill. A complete creature of habit, Amigo perked his ears as we turned the last corner, his objective coming into view. Sniffing the air for any news of the park's morning occupants, he shot a quick look in my direction before straining to reach the first of many trees. In spite of all my diligence, I've yet to communicate clearly to him that our walks are about the journey, not the destination.

For Amigo, our trip's itinerary consists of zigging and zagging his way from tree to shrub, sign post to rock, always favoring the exact spot he visited on the previous day's expedition. Not truly appreciating the joys of canine instinctual behavior, I offered to speed up this portion of our excursion with the command to "hurry up," but receiving in return that backward, over-the-shoulder glance which, if spoken by a human, would translate to "You talkin' to me?" Reminding myself that these daily rituals are not only pleasurable to a dog, but opportunities to further the bonding process between man and beast, I resisted the growing urge to yank on the leash and jar Amigo from his gratifying sniff-fest. My patience paying off in the end, we progressed another ten feet until the scent faded and a fresh canine-bouquet lured him forward.

Content with his inspection of the park grounds, Amigo nudged my leg with his cool, wet nose, indicating that he was finished with his duty and ready to proceed. Making our way to the frequently used path at the far end of the park, I noticed another dog walking his human. Judging from their speed, I estimated we were moments from a face-to-face encounter. Reigning in Amigo's lead, I stepped to the side and waited for the duo to pass. In the ensuing dog-dance required to enjoy the pleasure of canine communication, we managed to separate the dogs and put a few steps between us. Feeling resistance as I stepped forward, I realized that although Amigo's body was moving forward, his head was turned backward, still straining for one last sniff of the recently departed. Determined to enjoy our outing on this fine day, I continued walking several steps and then, "Whack!" Looking down to locate the origin of the noise, I realized Amigo had just smacked his head on the three foot post separating the park from the path. So intent on looking behind to scrutinize what had just passed by, he was oblivious to what lay ahead! After a good, hearty laugh I rubbed his head and carried on with the morning's walk.

Still smiling over the incident, I considered the lesson clearly set before me: Amigo doesn't have a vision problem, he has a focus problem. If he had been looking in the direction he was walking he would have avoided the post, altering his steps to the left or right. But the enticement of another canine sent him into a tail-spin and he completely lost his focus. Without concentration, any object in his path was a potential instrument of injury, pain or harm.

On any journey, there are certain rules of the road which must be not only observed but practiced, so that all who travel that path make it safely home. While most of us are willing, even diligent to comply with these rules, we sometimes neglect to apply this same model to our life's journey. Failing to stay focused on what really matters in life, we can find ourselves wounded emotionally or spiritually; wrecked and bleeding on the side of the road. Perhaps this is the reason the writer of the book of Hebrews, after encouraging us to lay aside whatever robs us of our potential to run the race set before us, follows with these words, "Let us fix our eyes on Jesus, the author and perfecter of our faith who for the joy set before Him endured the cross..." (Hebrews 12:2 NIV).

Lest we become discouraged by the obstacles which harm us and cause pain along our life's passage, we are left with these words about God who, during His earthly course, practiced the necessity of keeping His focus on the one thing that mattered: Our redemption.

About the Author

Daryl Knudeson works alongside her pastor-turned-military husband in both civilian and military communities. A speaker and Bible teacher, she has written Bible studies for women's interactive discussion groups and local church use. She has contributed articles for *InSpirit* magazine, a magazine for women, and the *Covenant Home Altar*—both international church publications. A portion of her writing is drawn from her travels and experiences working within the mission of International Renewal Ministries and Abide Ministries.

59433391R00109

Made in the USA
Charleston, SC
03 August 2016